for Judy

REFLECTIONS
FROM A
GARDEN

REFLECTIONS
FROM A
GARDEN

SUSAN HILL
&
RORY STUART

PAVILION

First published in Great Britain in 1995 by
PAVILION BOOKS LIMITED
26 Upper Ground, London SE1 9PD

Text copyright © Susan Hill and Rory Stuart 1995
Illustrations copyright © Ian Stephens 1995

Designed by David Fordham

The moral right of the authors has been asserted.

All rights reserved. No part of this publication may be reproduced,
stored in a retrieval system, or transmitted, in any form or by any means,
electronic, mechanical, photocopying, recording or otherwise,
without the prior permission of the copyright holder.

A CIP catalogue record for this book is available from the British Library.

ISBN 1 85793 395 8

The authors and publisher are grateful to the following for permission
to reproduce copyright material:
Faber and Faber Ltd for the extracts on pp. 9 and 87 from 'Burnt Norton'
by T. S. Eliot, taken from Collected Poems 1909–62 (by permission of the
Eliot Estate), and the extract on p. 167 from 'The Sunlight in the Garden'
by Louis MacNeice, taken from The Collected Poems of Louis MacNeice,
edited by E. R. Dobbs; Estate of Ursula Bethell for A. P. Watt Ltd for the extract
on p. 96 from 'Time' by Ursula Bethell; A. P. Watt Ltd on behalf of Michael Yeats
for the extract on p. 103 from 'Coole Park and Ballylee, 1931' by W. B. Yeats

Typeset by Dorchester Typesetting Group Ltd in Goudy Old Style 10/14pt
Printed and bound in Great Britain by Hartnolls

2 4 6 8 10 9 7 5 3 1

This book may be ordered by post direct from the publisher.
Please contact the Marketing Department.

CONTENTS

*An asterisk in the text indicates
a cross-reference to the Grumbling Appendix*

PRELUDE

THE MAN OF GOOD TASTE ENDEAVOURS
TO INVESTIGATE THE CAUSES OF THE PLEASURE
HE RECEIVES, AND TO INQUIRE WHETHER OTHERS RECEIVE
PLEASURE ALSO.

HUMPHRY REPTON,
Observations on the Theory and Practice of Landscape Gardening

PRELUDE

THE BACK END OF NOVEMBER and it has been quite remarkably cold: for over a week, the air has streamed icily down from Siberia and the countryside has been scoured bare by a bitter wind. Every night the temperature has dropped down hard as a stone into a well; every morning the grass has been white and bristle stiff and the branches of the trees furred with frost. The ground is too hard for digging or planting: bare-rooted trees and the roses, just delivered, have been heeled in, and that dull task was got over as quickly as possible. These are not days to linger out in the garden.

But then last night, the temperature rose a little, the wind eased back, so that now, of course, instead of frost there is fog, grubby and opaque, tasting unpleasantly metallic in the mouth, blotting out the light and the sky.

Light the fire early.

The best of the late garden jobs are all done. October was perfect for them, a month of golden days, crisp around the edges, the sky hard and blue, the sun a copper gong as it set. Bonfires with their nostalgic smell. Digging up the last of the potatoes on one cheerful Saturday, with a prize for the person who found the most bizarrely shaped Pink Fir Apple – a child can transform that into a creature with the help of a matchstick or two.

Apples. Picking them up and picking them over and carrying baskets of them in to store – but it has been an abundant year and plenty are left to lie on the grass and be enjoyed by the birds.

The leaves are raked into bags and left for the winter to get on with rotting them.

There has been some trimming and tidying: tender things have been wrapped, or tucked under cloches. Then, a last, fond look round.

Everything is bare. On these days you can see the beautiful bone structure of the garden; it is like a face with the hair tied tightly back. Colour no longer matters. There are molehills humped about the lawn, but they do not matter either. The birds have started coming to the table for food again and the mice are back in the house, living their scurrying, secret lives behind the wainscots.

Four o'clock, and the last pips of light are pressed out of the day. Draw the curtains. Tea and toast. Wedge another log on the fire.

It is time to reflect upon the garden, an afternoon to have a satisfactory pile of nursery catalogues on the small table just to hand and a second pile, of books, on the floor beside the chair. Going through seed and plant lists is one of the best sedentary garden pleasures, especially if you treat them quite disrespectfully, making question and exclamation marks, ticks and asterisks and comments in the margins and dog-ears of the page corners. So many new ideas present themselves, so much money might be spent, so many flights of fancy be indulged, on winter afternoons like this, and anything in the garden seems possible. Perhaps next year will be the one in which to embark seriously upon alpines, create a raised bed for lime-haters, make a pond . . . a wild-flower meadow . . . bog garden. Dream on.

It is a day for armchair garden-visiting, for ambling through the pages of some richly illustrated books, to be astonished, to admire, to envy, to criticize all those impossibly perfect places, with weedless soil, yew hedges, well-shaven lawns and exactly placed statuary, where everything flowers in harmony, the vegetables are colour-coded and there is a designer tool shed. Nothing like a bit of a sneer for lifting the spirits.

But there is plenty to inspire too, on this grey afternoon, plenty of beauty, plenty of glory in gardens all over the world, whose gates open with the pages of the books, haunting gardens of Japan and China, symbolic, strange, whose appeal lies in their untranslatable, untransferable otherness and whose lessons may be learned by heart, but never copied. Water gardens. Public gardens. Ostentatious gardens. Gardens on mountainsides, and in brilliantly bright countries. Historic gardens, town gardens, eccentric gardens, opulent gardens, hideous gardens. The images dazzle, overlap and confuse, the photographs are stagy, varnished, and sometimes vacuous, but every so often a page is turned and there the photographer has stood back quite self-effacingly, to let a garden itself show through and say what it has to; and from that page of the book, that garden on this November afternoon, who knows what inspiration and influence will quietly flow?

On a nearby shelf is a box of slides – photographs of gardens visited this past year. They may not match up to the glossy pictures of the professional photographers but they have a personal meaning missing from those, the element of memory. Browse through them and every so often pause, sit back. Remember. Gradually, with the photographs serving as a reminder, each visit, each particular garden, will separate itself from the rest and come vividly into focus and the days will come alive again. You can walk down the paths, turn corners, see those beautiful places in the mind's eye. And the pleasure is enhanced by the sudden recollection of small details, scarcely even connected with the plants or trees or beautiful vistas. Oh yes – *that* garden, where there was a cloudburst just as you were at the furthest point from any shelter. Look, here is the view of an inner courtyard glimpsed through a hole in an old stone wall. The photograph is inadequate, yet the calm and quiet and the unexpectedness of it can easily be recalled. Here, the roses were perfect; there, surely there should have been some water to enliven a pretty but somehow dull garden. Why is there a photograph of such an ugly summer house, such a disproportionately large urn, such a wearisome length of yew hedge? To serve as warnings,* just as the picture of a clematis spilling out of the confines of a stone trough will serve as an inspiration.

Some people file their photographs most efficiently, using these winter afternoons to bring the system up to date: others fish out, spread out, shuffle together again and shove everything back in higgledy-piggledy packets. But the pleasure the photographs give is a happy and profitable one no matter what.

Even on days like this, some gardeners will have spent an hour or two outside, or at least doing jobs in the greenhouse, those admirable people who count the day lost if they have not got their hands into the earth or around a stem, or at the very least a label and a ball of green twine. Others even make work, because they feel guilty if they do not; but it is not a moral issue, only a question of temperament.

Reflecting and planning are garden work too. There are plenty of notebooks to be flattened out from where they were rolled into a pocket and their hasty, abbreviated comments and rain-spattered memos deciphered. Gardens visited during the summer past. Shrub groupings, plantings that caught the eye, an unknown botanical name to check. Why this west-facing border or peony bed, walled kitchen garden or vista, terrace or water feature, in an Open Garden in Somerset or Cornwall or Gloucestershire was so pleasing and memorable.

Temperament also comes into the business of reviewing the past year in the garden, and making plans for the next. Some people are meticulous, keep intricately detailed diaries week by week, month by month, and go through them on just such an afternoon: MEMO: *plants 'a' and 'b' did well, but 'x' and 'y' did not succeed. Why? Cost out this, pull out that. Next March or May try so and so. Too many clashing colours here, some gaps there, not enough climbers, remember the soggy bit below the wall, something taller needed over here, perhaps turf over the big round flower bed that never gets enough sun? Move, cut back, divide . . .*

What does it matter if only one in ten ideas ever comes to fruition? Trying them out in theory is more than half the fun and you can make any number of mistakes with no harm done to the garden.

But above all, such a dismal afternoon is for remembering, and this year for remembering in particular one perfect garden day, when everything came exactly together, place, people, weather, and nothing went wrong. Such a day becomes richer as time and memory work upon it. Immediately it is over the details coagulate, there is only an overall impression lingering on the surface of the mind, a blur of sunshine and the sound of voices, of a great many people together in the garden, of

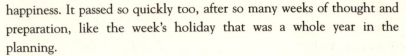

happiness. It passed so quickly too, after so many weeks of thought and preparation, like the week's holiday that was a whole year in the planning.

Yet such a day is altogether greater than the sum of its parts and, as it recedes in time, so individual elements separate themselves and find their own level of significance. Moments that flitted by are frozen now, arrested in the memory; the minutest incidents, an odd remark, a tiny visual pleasure, have been recorded for ever. The day is becoming clearer the further one moves away from it, and the pleasure of it is permanent and perpetual as it is recalled again and again on afternoons of winter succeeding one another for years to come. And the first of them is today.

Stir up the fire. Settle back. Close your eyes.

It is just beginning.

PERHAPS THE FIRST FEW MOMENTS after waking are the best of all, as on Christmas Day or a birthday in childhood. Lie still. Come to. Then, realize. It is here. It is today!

And, after all, the weather is to be perfect. It was a very warm night, the windows were left wide open and now, the pale dawn light before the sun rises has the opacity and sheen of the pods of honesty reflected on to the white wall.

There is a particular smell that is only smelt in the garden as early as this, before the night has altogether left it, and there are no distinct scents from individual flowers yet; they will only be released into the air later as the sun climbs and grows hotter. It will be evening when they smell headiest of all.

Get up, lean out of the window. There is only a damp, overall garden freshness, faintly steeped in rose petal and earth. The moles' mysterious tunnels have erupted all over the surface of the lawn.

From here, the little pond is out of sight, yet there is always a sense of it; because it is a living thing and constantly changing, something is always going on there. Just now, it will be the splash and splatter of the birds as they bathe in its shallows. If you glance quickly, perhaps there is a quick brilliance as the sunlight touches the drops shaken out from a hedge sparrow's wing.

Beyond the garden, over the hedge and far away, a line of soft vapour lies, marking the river. It would be beautiful down there, now: you might see dippers standing on their vantage stones in the middle, where the water runs shallow, and hear the peculiar whistle of the kingfisher, just before it flashes past, a sudden astonishing blue. But walking to the river across three fields takes half an hour – there is not time now, though later some of the children may go.

The birds have been singing since first light cracked open the eggshell of the sky, though they have passed their spring peak of ecstasy and their notes are softer now, they are less passionately strident.

The garden lies below and beyond the windows, contained, quiet. Expectant. There are beautiful shadows, the shapes of bushes and trees emerge, the light slips behind leaves and petals, picking them out. Later everything will seem to flatten and become picture-bright, with every outline hard under the high, bright midday sun. The garden always looks best very early and again later, when the evening shadows lie long, unsettling everything; and there is quite a different garden.

Two blackbirds panic out from beneath a bush. The cat is coming home, tail high, pricking delicately over the damp grass, mouse in mouth.

Downstairs to the dark, cool kitchen where the fridge hums and the clock ticks and night still lurks in the corners. Draw the bolt with a satisfying clunk. Open the back door and let the early morning slip with the cat into the kitchen. Step outside.

But leave the door open. It will stay open now until very late: indoors and out of doors will flow into one another all day with no break between them.

There is a sense of expectancy about the garden. It is waiting. The birds are very noisy though, as if they must get all their bustle and activity over with early, before it gets too hot.

It will be very hot. But for the moment, there is still a sweet coolness over the garden and the shadow of the house lies dark and strong across the grass.

It is a morning to have breakfast alone. There is a rickety old table on the veranda, and a wicker chair with faded cushions – they seem to have grown old with the house. Did they once belong to a great uncle? Who can remember? There is nothing smart about them but they are very comfortable; they will do for a good while yet.

For the rest of the day, food will be shared at a long, crowded, convivial table, with talk and shouts of laughter and the clatter of china. But now, there is time to savour the exquisite pleasure of being alone, eating and drinking alone, and of having the garden entirely to oneself. But first, take a colander and crunch down the gravel path that leads to the kitchen garden, for it is here that blueberries grow, a few bushes, in their self-contained bed – for this soil is lime; they would never grow in the ordinary way. Clouded blueberries and then raspberries, a handful of each, eaten with sugar and thin cream out of a blue bowl. Freshly ground coffee steams from its pot into a great mug and there is new brown bread and butter. And the swifts, screaming and swooping fast down into their nest under the eaves, and out again in one unbroken movement and away. The sun is up. The dew is off the grass. The great swags of the rose, 'Paul's Himalayan Musk', that covers the veranda and the sheds beside it, and the outhouse along from it, thick as clots of cream, are beginning to smell strongly. The great border is still in shade, not attracting much notice yet. But by eleven o'clock it will be in full, glorious sunlight, dramatic and costumed, waiting to be admired.

Scrape around the bowl to catch the last of the fruit-stained cream, enjoy the final mouthful of coffee.

Before everyone arrives, there are jobs to be done. The bees are moving already, busy over patches of clover. Time to get going.

Take a stiff broom to sweep the gravel off the terrace and some flotsam of twigs and soil from the edges of the path, enjoying the satisfying rasp of the bristles as they brush to and fro.

The garden needs crisping up a little, for it is going to be shown off today and this is a pleasant task for early in the morning, wandering about, bending down to deadhead, pull up a weed and admire something newly in flower. There are daisies on the lawn: some would get out the mower at once and off with their heads. But they are such modest, pretty things, turning their faces to the sun and it will please the children to make long, long daisy chains after lunch, picking out those whose petals are tipped with lipstick. In the shade, close to the tool shed, stands a young tree, still in its fat pot, to be planted ceremoniously this afternoon. Now it is time to give it a long drink, and get out the spade and wipe the blade carefully to make it shine. And there, hanging in the tool shed, is the edge cutter; so have it down and spend quarter of an hour slicing off the whiskery untidiness from around the flower beds – the gardening equivalent of cutting the loose pastry from around the edge of a pie, and every bit as satisfying.

This is gentle, restful gardening, nothing to make one hot or cross – not even very necessary; but it gives pleasure. As it does to plant out a few cuttings, fill up some gaps. The jobs occupy the hands but leave most of the mind free. They are being done to make the garden look nicer but none of them are chores. Now there are sounds coming from the kitchen. The helpers have arrived.

Already it is getting hot. The sun climbs higher and there is a silky look to the sky. But walk across the grass barefoot – it is quite dry now – to the pond, still cupped in shadow. Stand beside it and look down, down. But you cannot see anything below, only an insect drawing a skein across the smoothness. Bend and touch your hands to the water, feel it slip between dabbling fingers. By noon the surface will be warm under the full sun, and then you will have to dip your hand deeper to find the coolness, or go further to seek refreshment at the very bottom of the garden, for there, low down between grassy banks, the little stream runs through – though on these hot midsummer days it is shallow and trickles quite slowly over the stones. The children will clamber down and stand with bare feet in it, and leafy branches that overhang will brush against their heads and screen them from view. The stream is no trouble, makes no work, continues its own secret life – the most deeply satisfying thing in the garden.

A burst of laughter from the kitchen and then the crash of a plate on to the stone-flagged floor. Get out the chairs and set them up, pinching fingers as always between the flaps. Someone calls. So, down the path again to the kitchen garden, with basket and knife, to kneel among the tight-packed rows of brilliant green and pull lettuce and spring onions, pick off baby peas and tiny beans; the smell of the earth comes up with them. Into the greenhouse, where the shades are already down against the sun and the smell of tomatoes is pungent, dusky, evocative.

A car starts up, wheels spin on the gravel. Someone has gone off to the strawberry fields where the first fruit is ripening – though it will take hard searching to fill a basket – but still, it will be a pleasure too, for the field lies high up on a slope. From the top you look down on half the county, under the dissolving mist.

Take the basket into the kitchen, with a bunch of herbs for the salad. But they cry 'Shoo' and 'No room, no room'; you are bustled out from under their feet.

Go and stand beneath the weeping silver pear tree and look again towards the greater border; it is just emerging into the light of the full sun and perfect, the sweep of blues and white and cream and palest pink and deepest pink, merging into all the colours of fire, with delphiniums seven feet high and lupins that smell of pepper, great clumps of lilies. But in such a proud thing, it is not a matter of naming names or picking out this or that; the point of the great border is the whole, the balance of shapes, the blending of colours, the total effect and it will not matter that a person who stands before it later does not know the name of one single plant and cares less; they will gasp and enjoy and be satisfied none the less by the grand sight of it.

Just for a moment, there is not the slightest stirring in the air, everything is quite still. And so the garden seems perfectly suspended in time and space and you at the centre of it. *There is* no past or present, and the day to come waits in the wings.

> *Time past and time future*
> *What might have been and what has been*
> *Point to one end, which is always present.*

The light is clear, there is gilding drawn with a fine brush around the edges of things.

A thrush cracks a snail against a stone; and glancing down, you see the stumps of salvias that were planted out only yesterday, bleeding whitish green sap. The garden is no longer perfect then, nothing stays the same, and the light has changed again too, dappling over the trunks of the apple trees in the orchard, highlighting the pale-blue clematis on the far wall. If you half-close your eyes, the two merge together, making a pattern. The garden is always waiting to tell you something.

There is no moment like this, there will be none so exquisite, so intensely pleasurable, no matter the delights of the coming day, for now you have everything to yourself, you may hold on to it and, for a second, almost wish that no one would arrive and nothing would happen after all.

Too late, the first car has turned into the gate and others are coming up the lane. Too late to regret or even to repair the ravages of rabbits, too late for standing still. Everyone is arriving. It is now. The day has properly begun.

THERE ARE CHILDREN OF ALL AGES and all meld together and then come apart, to re-group, as they will continue to do, like the changing patterns in a kaleidoscope, throughout the day. There is only a little first shyness – most of them know each other and instant best-friendships are soon made. They pelt away, to the orchard, the stream, the nut walk, the stile that leads into the field, floppy hats discarded, dresses hitched up, shirts flying loose. Only one small boy lingers, face close pressed into his mother's skirt – but peeping out too, so that all at once he is off, waited for and following, burbling with laughter. To the children the garden is a backdrop, a playground, a mysterious or secret place: in the course of the day it will become a wild wood, a treasure island, a never-never-land, but never simply a garden. Beyond it, on the open area of grass that perhaps one day will be planned and planted and drawn into the rest, there will be cricket and croquet and a crazy kind of tennis over a clothes line, and energetic adults will join in. Now though, the adults are going around the garden, drinks in hand, some knowledgeably, some with cries of appreciation, surprise, recognition, some spilling out comparisons and botanical names; others silent, merely looking and enjoying. A few do not stir from the terrace; for them the garden is another kind of backdrop, pretty and pleasant but not of interest for itself. Some gardeners mind that, as mothers mind those who do not show interest in their children. But the garden, like the children, gives and means something different to everyone.

On the step are some plants in pots or carefully rolled in damp newspaper, offerings from other gardens, and this or that will be taken home in exchange, for gardeners are generous by nature, caretakers only of the things they grow; the best of them are quite unproprietorial.

Chairs are being brought out and the long table set up under the pergola and a great white cloth, only used for summer parties and for Christmas, is unrolled carefully, before the awning is raised – its whiteness dazzles too brightly under the sun. It is very hot; you would have to get right inside the bushes to find dark, dusty shade and there is no coolness, even down by the stream. There is a wonderful sensation of coolness near at hand, though. The pleasure that running, splashing water gives on these hot days is intense. Above a stone trough in which a slab of dark gleaming water rests quite still, a shell basin catches and, for a few seconds, holds it as it spews out of a lion's mouth. The sound refreshes and the sparkle of light as the sun touches the water gives *joie de vivre* to the garden.

Trays of glasses, diamond bright, plates of food, like painters' palettes, loaves, dishes of butter in ice, tender slices of meat and delicate fish, heaps of oily new potatoes pricked over with chives, bowls of glistering black olives, raspberries, strawberries, bilberries, cake and jugs of the creamiest cream. Sugar mountains. The chink of ice cubes in jugs of home-made lemonade and iced tea, droplets running down the cold bottles of very good white wine. Individual umbrellas are set up behind some of the chairs for the very old, and high chairs and wobbly piles of cushions for the very young. Bang a spoon on a tin can. 'Lunch, lunch.' Everyone comes tumbling.

And for a while, the garden is not taken notice of by anyone; except for the one whose garden this is, who looks up from a plate of crab to see the rose 'New Dawn' in full sun, full glory, every bud burst open and realizes that it has reached the attic windows and one morning soon will clamber in if something isn't done, and makes a tiny mental note to do it.

Otherwise the garden drowses, left to itself in the sun, and food and drink and talk take over. There is a great deal of merriment, a great deal of noise, and trays carried in and out and someone spills a glass and berry juice stains fingers and mouths and clothes, wine dark. The ice begins to melt. In the empty house, the cat has slunk upstairs to sleep a forbidden sleep on the best bed.

Soon others will sleep. The food is finished, talk peters out, the last glass is drained. The ice is a puddle of water at the bottom of the bucket. It is too hot. The garden looks exhausted, irritated by bees.

People move apart to lie in long chairs, on rugs, or the grass beneath the trees. The children have all gone down to the river and only the babies are left, peaceful in cribs. The host climbs into the hammock slung between two old perry pears and rocks very gently, unresistingly, to sleep.

There are places in the garden for everyone. Two of the young, who may be lovers, have wandered quietly down to the lake and untied the old boat and are paddling almost silently across to the little island, hands trailing like weeds in the water. No one knows. The children have begun to dam the stream.

The peak of the day is past while no one is looking. And then the sun begins its scarcely perceptible climb down the ladder of the afternoon.

No one wants to eat tea, but a cup is welcome and, after that, everyone must gather at the top of the garden; even the lovers come reluctantly from their island fastness. It is time to plant the commemorative tree. The hole was already dug out with much care yesterday and now the oldest and almost the youngest take hold of the new oak, while someone else helps to lift and settle it in. For a long time it will be small and uninteresting enough, with its rabbit-guard and its plain stake. But this is for the garden of the far future, a garden beyond your sight and planning.

It is done and firmed round, and one of the smallest boys has staggered up under the weight of a full watering can, stoutly spurning all offers to help; the earth and the roots are vigorously soaked. The tree is there for the rest of the lives of everyone here, and for generations to come. A silence falls: someone almost begins a speech – but does not; there is a little ripple of applause instead, and then time for more tea and a surprise cake – for which, after all, people do have room. But the children are gone, carrying baskets of old clothes and a peculiar assortment of items from the house, down to the clearing below the spinney, to practise a play amid whoops and giggles and a note from a tuneless pipe. The garden has become yet another place again, a theatre for changelings. The seats are set out in a different way and the adults become an audience. There is more suppressed laughter from the bushes. A pause. Someone half-emerges but is dragged back by a darting hand. 'Not yet!' A blackbird suddenly sets up singing from the lilac bush. And then, a small figure steps boldly out on to the stage, brandishing a sword.

The honeysuckle has begun to smell intoxicating and the roses and the stocks and the white lilies too. More birds start singing. The garden is coming alive again as the shadows deepen and spread and the light softens, silvering the trunk of the birch tree. The play proceeds; white flowers become translucent. In an hour or two they will be the ghosts of themselves. The children are all there now, clustered together on the stage, all singing. Then, for a second, they fall shyly silent, and bring the watchers to the unexpected edge of tears, as such moments do. We shall remember this and know as much.

A small boy says quietly, 'I saw the lake. It has gone black.'

One of the babies begins to cry, a child trips over the dressing-up cloak, and fractiousness, like a sort of teething, unsettles the mood.

Time to start for home. It is over, it is nearly over.

Goodbyes. Good wishes. Laughter. Crying. The cars start up.

Wave. Then wait until it is quite still again.

The table stands bare. Chairs tucked neatly in. The helpers are long gone. Stand at the top of the rise and look down on the garden. It is all in shadow now, retreating gradually back into itself. Turn. Look up and see the full moon come sailing up the sky and hang there. Turn again. In the west, the sky is still poppy red and crimson where the sun has set. Over the field the owls will skim soon; the badgers will stumble out of the woods, and the hedgehog snuffle along the bottom of the ditch.

It is time to repossess the garden. Time to take a watering can quietly round. Every garden smell rises fresh and distinct to the nostrils. The frogs plop, breaking the surface of the little pond.

The shapes of shrubs and trees change now, some recede, others loom larger. The honesty is paper-pale as the face of the full moon, the thistles silver as steel and Miss Willmott's ghost haunts the garden.

Then, it is beautiful and infinitely sad; then, the sense of the fleeting present and the solitude that is at the dark heart of the garden is suddenly acute.

But after all it was a perfect day.

Sit on the low wall and let everything sink down around you and the memory of everything that has happened settle on the spirit. The very beginning and the very end of it, alone in the garden, are the very best of all.

And last thing, before going up to bed, let out the cat, who will stand for a moment, ears pricked, tail waving a warning, before slipping, sleek and secretive and purposeful, out and away, into the night garden.

CHAPTER ONE

THEN SHE SET TO WORK NIBBLING AT THE MUSHROOM (SHE HAD KEPT A PIECE OF IT IN HER POCKET) 'TIL SHE WAS ABOUT A FOOT HIGH: THEN SHE WALKED DOWN THE LITTLE PASSAGE; AND *THEN* – SHE FOUND HERSELF AT LAST IN THE BEAUTIFUL GARDEN, AMONG THE BRIGHT FLOWERBEDS AND THE COOL FOUNTAINS.

LEWIS CARROLL
Alice in Wonderland

VISIONS

W E MAY FIND THE PERFECT GARDEN FIRST, not in life but
in books, and the pleasure of such imaginary gardens is
eternal, for they are not withered by winter nor
desiccated by drought; nor are they subject to the sway
of time or to our own ageing. When we enter and explore them, we fall
under their spell, and we may walk there again whenever we choose and
find them quite unchanged, though our view of them may alter as we
become more knowledgeable about real gardens and are able to fill out
half-imagined beds and borders for ourselves. They are gardens not in
isolation but in context of course, peopled by imaginary characters and
often having a very real purpose within the plot, rather than merely
prettily described scenery.

In the books of childhood, gardens are places of mystery, and
sometimes menace, full of long shadows and paths that twist out of sight
and, most delightful of all, secrets; they satisfy our early love of places
come upon by chance, on the other side of a plain door, over a hedge or
a long high wall, glimpsed tantalizingly, speculated upon deliciously,
before being daringly penetrated. The best of them are always forbidden
gardens.

The charm as well as the lurking threats of the kitchen garden are realized very early indeed in the life of those who come to Beatrix Potter's stories in the nursery. In her gardens, we are set firmly on the side of the animals, whose proper homes, not to say larders, we believe they should rightly be; human owners are giants who threaten and trample with great boots and human gardeners are to be both feared and teased, figures of doom, sentries and conquerors, full of pride and cruelty when rejoicing over their ill-gotten territories and their domination over the small, furry creatures.

> *Peter, who was very naughty, ran straight away to Mr McGregor's garden, and squeezed under the gate! First he ate some lettuces and some French beans and then he ate some radishes; and then, feeling rather sick, he went to look for some parsley. But round the end of a cucumber frame, whom should he meet but Mr McGregor!*

There are few phrases so evocative of the Victorian and Edwardian kitchen garden as 'cucumber frame'. Who has one now? And though, as we grow up and become gardeners we may have a sneaking sympathy for Mr McGregor,* who 'jumped up and ran after Peter, waving a rake and calling out, "Stop, thief!"' the small child within us is secretly for ever on the side of the marauding young rabbit.

Beatrix Potter's world is that of the country house or cottage garden giving straight on to the open fields and woods, which creep right up to the gate and are full of dark terrors and potential violence. Within the garden itself, securely fenced, all is order and neatness, with cabbages and lettuces in regimentally straight rows. Kitchen gardens may have shrunk in size, but any nostalgia we may have for the Victorian and Edwardian style surely leads back to *The Tale of Peter Rabbit*, whose pictures reflect a perfect world of long wooden rakes and besom brooms, sturdy green metal watering cans and tall clay celery forcing pots stacked inside potting sheds. Here, red geraniums grow in plant pots up the steps and sieves have wooden rims; gooseberries are netted the old-fashioned way. It is an ordered, happy world, but it is also a world quite realistic about the natural violence of things. As adults we long to return to it; as children we are half enthralled and half alarmed by its underlying threat.

The best gardens are never revealed to us all at once; there is always mystery, always something leading us on to the unexpected, always surprise, and perhaps the gardens that tantalize us, first and last, real and imaginary, are inaccessible – either temporarily or for ever. The very pleasure of a garden in fiction is that we can never attain it, never penetrate it – because it does not exist. As children we may have stood looking through a locked gate into a forbidden garden. As adults, the glimpse through a gap in the hedge appears to reveal a magical one, but our way is barred by the sign that says *Private*. There is positively no garden more longed for than the one whose only Open Day in the year we have just missed, few garden pleasures more delicious than that of being granted private access on a closed day, when we have the garden to ourselves and our enjoyment is enhanced by the knowledge that we alone are privileged to be inside the gates and all others must press their noses against them in vain.

Of course, our own gardens are never inaccessible to us, but we may try to imitate the effect of closed worlds by skilful use of gates and spyholes affording glimpses of the view ahead, holes cut in hedges, narrow paths that apparently lead to dead ends, only to turn at the very last minute and open out into a delightful space. And to anyone who reads *Alice in Wonderland* as a child, the frustration of being barred from a beautiful garden seen through a narrow perspective, and the joy of finally gaining entrance are already very familiar.

> Alice opened the door and found that it led into a small passage, not much larger than a rat-hole. She knelt down and looked along the passage into the loveliest garden you ever saw. How she longed to get out of the dark hall and wander about among those beds of bright flowers and those cool fountains. But she could not even get her head through the doorway. 'Oh, how I wish I could shut up like a telescope!'

Alice's cry is the eternal one of the adult longing to shrink back through size and time into childhood again and so gain entry to the garden whose delights of 'bright flowers and cool fountains' contrasted with the small dark hall are so perfectly and simply summed up. When we make our gardens are we only ever trying to re-create Arcadia and the Land of Lost Content?

The garden Alice finally gets into is a strange, surrealistic one, a place of the dream that borders on nightmare, where playing-card gardeners, in fear of being beheaded, paint white roses red, and croquet is played on the lawns with hedgehogs for hoops and flamingos held by the feet for mallets. There is only dementia here and endless illogical argument and the garden Alice enters through the looking glass is little better – all pert talking flowers and front paths that lead you in the opposite direction to the house. It fascinates us yet, either as children or as adults, we would feel uneasy at the prospect of actually going there.

The 'Secret Garden' of Frances Hodgson Burnett's classic children's novel is a very different matter, perhaps the most ideal and longed for garden of all. Young Mary Lennox, a sour, pale, solitary child, is orphaned in India and sent to the bleak Misselthwaite Manor belonging to her godfather, high on the Yorkshire Moors. There, at least at first, her isolation is absolute; she has no playmates and her only companions are servants, friendly in a gruff and forthright Yorkshire way but too busy to spend much time with her. She passes hours walking round and round the paths of the bare winter gardens alone, but one day Martha the maid mentions in passing that 'One of the gardens is locked up. No one has been in it for ten years.' At first Mary finds the idea unimaginable, and unappealing too, for her experience of gardens up until now has been a miserable one. Yet in spite of herself she is intrigued.

> She could not help thinking about the garden which no one had been into for ten years. She wondered what it would look like and whether there were any flowers still alive in it. When she had passed through the shrubbery gate, she found herself in great gardens, with wide lawns and winding walks with clipped borders. There were trees, and flowerbeds, and evergreens clipped into strange shapes, and a large pool with an old grey fountain in its midst. But the flowerbeds were bare and wintry and the fountain was not playing. This was not the garden which was shut up. How could a garden be shut up? You could always walk into a garden.

And now begins one of the finest pieces of garden writing in all fiction – as well, perhaps, as a marvellous kind of garden designing. Frances

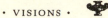

Hodgson Burnett knows exactly how to lead the reader along, deeper and deeper into the mystery of the garden, plotting tensely all the way as Mary presses forward. First, she follows a path, at the end of which 'there seemed to be a long wall, with ivy growing over it'. In the wall she finds a green door – it is open and she can go through, so 'this was not the closed garden evidently'. This walled garden 'was only one of several which seemed to open into one another'.

As we accompany Mary, we read with mounting excitement, which is checked once again, for next we come to 'another open door, revealing bushes and pathways between beds containing winter vegetables. Fruit trees were trained against a wall and over some of the beds there were glass frames.'

And if we delight in that sort of garden and are ready to be ravished by it, we receive another check. 'The place was bare and ugly enough, Mary thought, as she stood and stared about her. It might be nicer in summer, when things were green. But there was nothing pretty about it now.'

Our enthusiasm having been doused with this, we are now ready to encounter with Mary one of the long line of fictional gardeners who are professional curmudgeons. 'He had a surly old face and did not seem at all pleased to see her.' (Later, the gardener's crusty exterior flakes away and he becomes Mary's friend and ally. But she has to win his friendship slowly, the hard way, as she still has to discover and win entry to the secret garden.)

A second green door, more walls and winter vegetables and glass frames. A second wall. On we trudge. And then – surely, surely – 'In the second wall there was another green door: and it was not open.'

It never fails to make the heart stop just for a second, no matter how many times we have come to it, and we are one with Mary as she goes to the door and turns the handle 'hoping that the door would not open, because she wanted to be sure she had found the mysterious garden'.

But again we are thwarted. The door opens easily into an orchard with 'bare fruit trees growing in the winter-browned grass' and no green door to be seen anywhere. Disappointment.

Then Mary notices that the far wall does not seem to end with the orchard, 'but to extend beyond it as if it enclosed a place at the other side'. And indeed it does. But on that first day, we are not allowed a sight of it and only given the feeling that Mary has so strongly of its presence on the other side of the wall. Weeks have to pass, during which she comes to know the gardener, Ben Weatherstaff, and hovers about near the wall, as winter turns imperceptibly towards spring. The plot then takes a turn down an apparently unrelated path and several dramatic events almost distract Mary's and the reader's attention from any thought of the garden – almost, but not quite. The weather changes again and becomes less grim, the year moves further towards spring and then Mary encounters a tame robin, and the robin shows her the newly turned patch of earth in which he has been scratching for a worm and found, instead, a key – the key to the garden?

It is indeed, and the climax to Mary's quest, when it comes, is breathtaking, delightful and wholly satisfying. Yet almost better than the description of the real Secret Garden, when she finds it, and as spring and summer flush it with first growth, are the last few moments when it is still unseen, unpenetrated, unexplored.

> She put the key in and turned it. It took two hands to do it, but it did turn.
>
> And then she took a long breath and looked behind her up the long walk to see if anyone was coming. No one was coming. No one ever did come, it seemed, and she took another long breath, because she could not help it, and she held back the swinging curtain of ivy and pushed back the door which opened slowly – slowly.
>
> Then she slipped through it, and shut it behind her, and stood with her back against it, looking about her and breathing quite fast with excitement, and wonder, and delight.
>
> She was standing inside the secret garden.

After that, beautiful though the garden is, and symbolic of the story as it unfolds, the strangeness and the waiting, the mystery and the sense of heart-stopping anticipation are over; as the garden is entered and becomes known, and carefully described – *gardened*, its magic is somehow lost: until we pick up the book again and embark upon the same, extraordinary journey.

From time to time there are attempts to construct the real Secret Garden in imitation of and homage to the book: designers have imagined it, and had their plans carried out for one or other of the flower shows where ephemeral gardens are created. It is a pretty idea and they have been pretty gardens, but they are not and can never be the Secret Garden, whose essential mystery could never be actualized, partly because its very essence was age – it was quite overgrown, a garden whose door had been locked and the key to that door buried for ten years. Impossible to bring such age and neglect and tangled undergrowth, in which lie so many hidden plants, artificially forth; wrong, and against the spirit of the story; wrong, above all, because it never was or could be a real garden at all.

Tom's 'Midnight Garden' is even less 'real', not only because it is fictional, a garden in the classic novel for children by Philippa Pearce, but also because it is a garden out of real time. During an enforced stay with a dull uncle and aunt Tom hears the grandfather clock strike thirteen; on getting out of bed to explore, he finds a door that leads not to the bit of yard backed by a wall which he has been led to expect, but into a quite different place.

> A great lawn where flowerbeds bloomed; a towering fir tree, and
> thick, beetle-browed yews that humped their shapes down two sides
> of the lawn; on the third side, to the right, a greenhouse, almost
> the size of a real house; from each corner of the lawn, a path that
> twisted away to some other depths of garden, with other trees.

On this first, astonishing night Tom only looks at the garden and the next day, in ordinary clock time, finds merely the yard he was told about; but on the second night he gets up and goes out at the 'time between night and day when landscapes sleep' and then he enters the garden. It is quite magically described, a still, breathtaking, mysterious place, out of time, a dream garden and yet recognizable too. Here are not the talking flowers or painted roses of Alice's Wonderland; this is recognizable and traditional, with all the features of the classic and mature country house garden of Victorian and Edwardian England; and beyond it is the countryside, meadows where sheep and cattle graze, a river, the blue hills.

The atmosphere of the garden is inextricably bound up with that of the story: for this is a book about the interweaving of past with present, nostalgia, the mysterious nature of time and the sadness of human change and ageing. The garden is there and not there, already part of a vanished past and yet accessible through dreams and magic time-displacement – old, calm, handsome, in some ways a very serious and solemn place, which has the same effect upon Tom as would some great, ancient, empty cathedral: he feels amazement and awe, he is silenced and slightly puzzled. Yet the garden welcomes his youthful boyishness too – there are trees to climb, particularly a huge yew, nooks and crannies to explore, fruit to be scrumped and surreptitiously eaten.

These are so often the gardens we refer to in our imaginations, when we become adults and make our own; it is not that we wish to copy them in every detail, though we may always desire to incorporate special elements – hiding places, doors in walls, secret gardens-within-gardens, pools, old potting sheds, high, dark hedges, paths winding mysteriously away, sudden glimpses of the open fields stretching beyond, scented flowers, sparkling fountains, old trees for climbing. It is their atmosphere we most long to re-create and recapture and with it our own sense of past childhood.

Old gardens are so often evocative places, redolent of the past, and the ghosts of those who have worked and walked there. And the desire, either to take over an existing garden or to establish one containing the things we somehow feel are necessary to help us recapture childhood feelings, is very strong in us. When contemporary garden designers complain, and rightly, about the lack of interest in striking modern garden designs, they are expressing their frustration at having to contend both with the taste of garden owners and makers and with this deeply rooted garden tradition, expressed not only in real gardens but in fictional ones, and especially in books from the golden age of children's literature. Not for nothing is Humphrey Carpenter's definitive account of the late Victorian and Edwardian era in children's writing called *Secret Gardens*.

We yearn for the gardens that never were, of our early reading, as for the lost happiness of childhood itself. If we cannot grow smaller, like

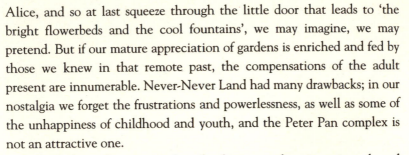

Alice, and so at last squeeze through the little door that leads to 'the bright flowerbeds and the cool fountains', we may imagine, we may pretend. But if our mature appreciation of gardens is enriched and fed by those we knew in that remote past, the compensations of the adult present are innumerable. Never-Never Land had many drawbacks; in our nostalgia we forget the frustrations and powerlessness, as well as some of the unhappiness of childhood and youth, and the Peter Pan complex is not an attractive one.

Nevertheless, the sense of exile from paradise is universal and expressed most vividly in the poetry and metaphor of the Bible, whose image of heaven is a garden and whose verses are thick with references to gardens as places of refreshment and peace, coolness and shade. Genesis gives us very few props and yet they are quite sufficient for us to design our vision of the Garden of Eden.

Water came first: until it did 'there was neither shrub nor plant growing wild upon the earth', and the water formed a river to flow through the garden. There were trees, for the beauty of their form and for their fruits; there was green grass. Then into the garden came living creatures who, in that most delectable and enticing of phrases, 'heard the sound of the Lord God walking in the garden in the cool of the evening'. No more is needed.

In his *Paradise Lost*, Milton cannot resist embellishing the Garden of Eden with 'flowers of all hue and without thorn the rose', lawns, a waterfall cascading into a lake, fields full of gently grazing sheep. But pleasing though they are in themselves, really such details are superfluous, for we make paradise for ourselves in our own imaginations, our own gardens.

But if it is to literature that we still look for inspiration, we will find paradise in the least serious places:

'For Wodehouse there has been no Fall of Man. The gardens of Blandings Castle are the original Garden of Eden from which we are all exiled.' Evelyn Waugh has put his finger on one of the most significant reasons for the success and persistent appeal of the novels of P. G. Wodehouse. Not only had he a consummate mastery of all the subtleties and humorous possibilities of the language he used so wonderfully, not only are the novels, soufflés though they may seem to be, among the funniest ever written; the idyllic world portrayed in them is indeed a paradise, though not so much lost as quite fictitious.

The world of Blandings Castle, seat of the ninth Earl of Emsworth, is one of pure and complete innocence; of young hearts sundered in springtime and reunited by midsummer, butlers bearing silver salvers laden with tea or telegrams across emerald velvet lawns to those seated in the shade of the cedar tree, of long hot summers and trysts at evening in dew-drenched rose gardens, conversations overheard by interlopers hidden in the shrubbery, pigs being fattened up for the county agricultural and dahlias for the horticultural shows. The setting is English, rural, timeless and perfect. There is the castle itself, 'huge and grey and majestic, flanked by rolling parkland and bright gardens and the lake glittering in the foreground'. And naturally, 'on a knoll overlooking the lake there stood a little sort of imitation Greek temple'. The soil is gravel, the climate perfect; there are spacious acres with mature trees perfectly kept; the rose gardens are the finest in England, beds and borders immaculate as a result of the endless work of teams of gardeners and under gardeners and gardeners' boys; views are impressive, seats in the shade to be found everywhere, tennis courts provided for the amusement of the young. There may be plots and machinations – and gardeners, of course, are always obstructive and surly – but nothing at Blandings succumbs to blight or mildew, the roses do not suffer from greenfly or blackspot, late frosts never blacken nor gales fell, and though summer days are hot, the greenness of the gardens never fades in any drought – the occasional timely thunderstorm provides a refreshing shower of rain exactly when needed.

In Lord Emsworth's garden there is open visiting for us, we may enter the grounds at will, wander freely and stay as long as we please. No signs read PRIVATE or KEEP OFF THE GRASS. We are as much lords of these parks, grounds, gardens and messuages as the noble inhabitants.*

Garden fashions change very slowly and some styles have never been completely lost – they represent a sort of desirable state to us, one which, however falsely, we associate with an ideal way of life. Just such a garden is beautifully described by George Eliot in her novel, *Scenes of Clerical Life*. Interestingly, the narrator refers to it as:

One of those old fashioned paradises which hardly exist any longer except as memories of our childhood: no finical separation between flower and kitchen garden there; no monotony of enjoyment for one sense to the exclusion of another but a charming paradisiacal mingling of all that was pleasant to the eye and good for food. The rich flower border running along every walk, with its endless succession of spring flowers, anemones, auriculas, wall flowers, sweet williams, campanulas, snap-dragons and tiger lilies had its taller beauties such as moss and Provence roses, varied with espalier apple trees; the crimson of a carnation was carried out in the lurking crimson of the neighbouring strawberry beds; you gathered a moss rose one moment and a bunch of currants the next; you were in a delicious fluctuation between the scent of jasmine and the juice of gooseberries. Then what a high wall at one end, flanked by a summer house so lofty, that after ascending its long flight of steps you could see perfectly well that there was no view worth looking at; what alcoves and garden seats in all directions; and along one side what a hedge, tall and firm and unbroken like a green wall!

Many, if asked to describe the perfect garden, would come up with a close approximation to that one – the English cottage garden has in fact always existed and is a much-imitated style.

But we love the gardens of literature not primarily for themselves, or even as inspiration, but because of what happens in them, the part they play in a novel, the background setting they provide to the characters, their activities and inner feelings. Gardens have long been the trysting places of fiction, in which the first intimations of affection are stirred and the subject of love and marriage broached; women and men wait in them in trepidation and sometimes deep distress, momentous conversations take place there, so that ever afterwards we will picture those scenes in the gardens we have created with our inner eye: such places matter to us; we feel we know them as intimately as the characters of Henry James's *Portrait of a Lady* or Elizabeth Bowen's *The Last September*.

Sometimes, so much emotion fills a garden during a fictional encounter that it impresses us with particular force. In Charlotte Brontë's *Jane Eyre* the heroine has a meeting of great significance with Mr Rochester in the garden at Thornfield Hall – at evening, that most evocative and charged of times.

> *I went apart into the orchard. No nook in the grounds more sheltered and more Eden-like; a very high wall shut it out from the court on one side; on the other a beech avenue screened it from the lawn. At the bottom was a sunk fence, its sole separation from lonely fields: a winding walk, bordered with laurels and terminating in a giant horse chestnut, circled at the base by a seat, led down to the fence. Here one could wander unseen. While such honeydew fell, such silence reigned, such gloaming gathered, I felt as if I could haunt such shade forever; but in treading the flower and fruit parterres at the upper part of the enclosure, enticed there by the light the now rising moon cast on this more open quarter, my step is stayed – not by sound, not by sight, but once more by a warning fragrance. Sweetbriar and southernwood, jasmine, pink and rose have long been yielding their evening sacrifice of incense: this new scent is neither of shrub nor flower; it is – I know it well – it is Mr Rochester's cigar.*

A scene of this kind is moving and powerful in the context of the novel and lodges itself in the depths of the memory and the imagination: our experience of gardens in real life is made more vivid and significant, perhaps for ever afterwards, by the additional meaning and symbolism of fictional reference.

Fictional gardens, in books which mean much to us, become part of our imagination and memory. We visualize them in detail and endow them with personal significance; their atmosphere remains with us, deep in the subconscious memory. And buried with them is an expectation not only of what a garden should look like but what it should give to us. We recognize it at once when we meet it in real life and half-consciously strive to achieve it when creating our own gardens.

Most important of all, we feel a sense of absolute rightness when we are enclosed within a garden, held in its embrace. But as well as this comfortable sense of enclosure, we need the frisson of the unexpected, the feeling that paths may lead anywhere, and there may be danger lurking in the shrubbery and the shadows. But it is danger of a controlled, exciting, yet ultimately unthreatening kind. The woods may hide the gingerbread house of the witch, yet we know that the fairytale has a happy ending.

Because meetings and partings, often of great significance, take place in fictional gardens, we like those private corners, where two may be together and the air become highly charged with all manner of emotion. Such events may never take place in our more prosaic lives, but the place will suggest the possibility, which in itself adds spice to our routine days.

The gardens which appeal to us most have secret places, romantic places, mysterious places. They are also generally a little untidy, often neglected and wildly overgrown; and ruined gardens are perhaps the most appealing of all.

The gardens we read about and inhabit early in life, in our imaginations, may stimulate a love of them and a desire to make our own; and memory of fictional gardens will inform the ones we create and add another dimension of meaning to our delight in them.

Yet too much indulgence in our nostalgia can make us prey to sentimentality and backward looking, at the expense of fresh ideas and visions. We may yearn for a paradise garden and carry a longing to recreate an Eden deep within us. And that will sustain us and give life and meaning to our garden-making, so long as we look forward as well as back, and are open to the possibility that paradise may lie elsewhere than in the gardens of the golden afternoon of pre-1914, fictional England.

CHAPTER TWO

I HAVE A NEW GARDEN,
AND NEW IS BEGUN;
SUCH ANOTHER
KNOW I NOT UNDER SUN.

Anonymous

BEGINNINGS

'GARDENERS ARE BORN NOT MADE' is scarcely true at all. A few are. Green fingers do sometimes run in families. They are inherited by those small children who come from a long line of natural, instinctive and dedicated growers and who spend hours pottering quietly about alongside father, grandfather or aunt, being given small, pleasant tasks; they check the daily progress of seeds they themselves helped to sow, or the young vegetable plants they carried from greenhouse to nursery bed, learning in the best way of all, by looking, listening, being shown and copying. They may not always become garden makers, but they will be real, true growers, and frequently allotment owners and prize vegetable rearers.

On the whole, though, young children do not find gardening of much interest, for all the passing charms of the mustard and cress flannel, the classroom bean jar or the giant sunflower race. From time to time, books appear containing elaborate and optimistic advice for inspiring the tots by helping them create a *Peter Rabbit* or *Alice in Wonderland* themed garden plot.

Adults are the only ones who fall readily in love with this sort of thing. The young lose such mild interest as was drummed up in them after a week, as they do in the prettily packaged herb and cottage flower garden kits foisted on them at Christmas.

Nevertheless, articles still pop up as regularly and optimistically as daisies on the lawn on how to initiate the under tens into the magic world of making things grow.

The redoubtable Miss Gertrude Jekyll once wrote an entire book called *Children and Gardens*. Her nannyish tones ring through the prose as one can only too well imagine they once rang through the shrubbery.

> *A good straight bit of digging in clear ground for half an hour at a time will both soon train young hands and arms and backs . . . When you have a lunch at the playhouse you will want a nice salad, so I will tell you the right way to make it . . . Don't be afraid of the word 'botany'.*

But she is also the purveyor of some doughty common sense, practical and straight talking, never patronizing to the young. And although they themselves are unlikely to want to read it, her book is still of immense use to any adults who do come into contact with those rare creatures, keen child gardeners. She is particularly sound on the importance of encouraging, not deterring them, by giving them what they deserve – a decent piece of ground they can call their own, not some sour, starved corner close to a hedge and rejected by the adults; and decent equipment with which to work, not nasty, garish, plastic toys.

'I much doubt whether good small tools can be bought ready made,' she writes. They still cannot. 'What are kept in ironmongers shops as "ladies' tools" with varnished handles and blue blades and that are usually given to children, are wretched things – badly shaped, badly balanced and generally weak where they should be strongest.'*

If gardening does not get to very many people in childhood, it would seem even less likely to appeal to them in adolescence and certainly most teenagers find a garden only of interest as a pleasant space in which to drape themselves. Adults do not help by seeing them merely as a handy source of cheap labour. ('Two quid to mow the grass?')

But, in fact, horticulture is an increasingly popular career, good for those practical young to whom desk and paperwork are anathema and one of the areas in which apprentice jobs are still available and there is a

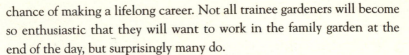

chance of making a lifelong career. Not all trainee gardeners will become so enthusiastic that they will want to work in the family garden at the end of the day, but surprisingly many do.

So where, and how, and why does it all begin? Usually when it has to. The gardening writer Ursula Buchan has shrewdly pointed out that what makes gardeners of most people is a mortgage. Notoriously, tenants of rented properties very often neglect the garden, but becoming a house owner will usually mean becoming a garden owner too. And so, a new world opens up. At first, and especially if the whole business is quite new to you, gardening may well be just one more job to add to a list – decorating, cleaning, washing, cooking. If you have moved into your house during the late autumn and winter there will be a few quiet months before you notice that there is an overgrown hedge to be clipped, grass to be mown and beds matted with weeds to be cleared. Perhaps a fence is broken and a back gate hangs askew – it is all rather depressing, but you will do the work because, having bought the place, you are as garden proud as you are house proud – perhaps even more, because the garden is on public view and understandably you do not want it to look unkempt and overgrown. But at this stage, knowing virtually nothing about gardens, you are still quite uncommitted to them and may remain so, for a time, for some years, perhaps for ever. Your garden will simply be there as a pleasant background to family and domestic life, the home of the washing line, the bicycle shed, the swing and the sandpit.

One day, however, something may happen and you will find yourself being nudged gently forwards, a step at a time, until you are standing on the brink of a transformation. From being simply a garden owner, you may become a gardener.

The transformation takes place by scarcely perceptible stages and it often begins in the most straightforward and matter-of-fact way of all. With vegetables.

Greed may be at the root of it, in the usual sense and in the form of a well-fed conscience and a starved bank balance. You have only to eat Sunday lunch at a house where the cook goes out to pick the vegetables seconds before they are in the saucepan and minutes before they come in dishes steaming to the table, to realize that absolutely fresh potatoes and peas, broccoli and beans are incomparably the sweetest, the most tender, and the most full of flavour – not to mention nutrients. When you return home that afternoon you may very well walk outside and begin to cast an eye around your own garden to see where you might site a vegetable plot.

Because of the outlay on tools and equipment, fertilizer and slug pellets, seeds and plants, the initial cost of producing home-grown vegetables to feed a family may not be very low. But it comes down dramatically every season and you can never put a price upon the satisfaction of making good use of the earth. Those who have strange twinges of conscience about spending time, money and the good ground simply on the decorative will sleep more soundly if they grow food as well.

Vegetable growing is hard work and you may begin dutifully but without much anticipation of pleasure. Pleasure there is, though, and deep satisfaction. You buy some seed potatoes and set them out to sprout on your window ledge. You dig a trench, place the potatoes in carefully, cover them with earth, and each week you pile more earth over the emerging shoots until you have several rows of neat mounds, dark and shapely as Toblerone chocolate. If you have picked up a bit of garden lore, you will have followed it for fun and planted your seed potatoes out on Good Friday. Three months later you begin to probe a fork gently about in the soil and for every potato planted you will very likely bring up half a dozen perfect new ones. They smell indescribable, damp, sweet, earthy. You cook them. And just as your newborn child is the most rare and beautiful ever to be seen in this world, so your potatoes taste better than any other potatoes in the history of eating.

The experience may not in itself be sufficient to transform you into the Compleat Gardener – but it is one of the most important of pleasures and it will almost certainly give you a taste for the business of growing.

Now a number of things may happen.

You may indeed be a grower – a vegetable grower, and the rest of the garden may gradually be eaten up by the vegetable plot as you become an enthusiastic provider of produce for your own family and half your friends and relations. From here, it is often a small step to becoming a *prize* vegetable grower, an exhibitor at the September horticultural show in the parish hall, the secret of whose giant onions is eagerly sought after. What began as a means to the simple end – providing enough fresh vegetables to feed your family regularly, cheaply and well – becomes an end in itself.

If you become a kitchen gardener on this scale, flowers will always be subservient to vegetables and at first you may well not grow any at all – peas and beans and carrots and cabbages will consume all your time and ground, energy and interest. But one of the reasons you have become a vegetable gardener may be the sight of the kitchen garden next door. A perfectly arranged plot of the old-fashioned kind such as your eighty-year-old neighbour tends is one of the most delightful and gratifying sights in gardening. Indeed, for this reason alone, the contemporary fashion for the highly formal, ornamental vegetable gardens, which it is *de rigueur* to call 'potagers',* is difficult to comprehend. Recondite varieties of lettuce, miniature cabbages, artichokes and chard are grown for their prettiness and colour-matching properties, and utilitarian, ugly vegetables (however delicious to eat) are rigorously excluded; the whole arrangement is preciously trimmed with low box hedging and impractical little cordons of step-over apples. Yet nothing could be more satisfying to the eye, and sensible and practical too, than the sort of kitchen garden from which Beatrix Potter's ferocious Mr McGregor was so intent on excluding Peter Rabbit. Such plots may be seen on half the allotments of Britain and in any village which still has a senior generation of local inhabitants in cottages and council houses. In spring and summer the impeccably hoed rows of feathery carrots and sturdy onions, potatoes under their ancient burial mounds of brown earth, and vivid green peas and Cos lettuce lined up like guardsmen are a joy to behold. Everything is neat, everything is orderly, everything is in its proper place. And at the head, a wigwam of runner beans stands sentinel, its flowers as scarlet as tunics. The lines of such gardens, made with dibber and tightened string, are perfectly straight, though softened as the season progresses by the shapes of the foliage, and there will be upturned pots for forcing rhubarb, some nice triangular cloches and a velvet parsley hedge.

To have such a vegetable garden next door to your own is more than likely to be an inspiration and you will also discover that the gardener who tends it is generally to be seen in it and always glad of a chat. In no time at all, and especially between the months of June and September, you will find fresh produce pressed upon you – lettuces in your porch, a marrow or some runner beans or a paper bag of tomatoes passed across the fence. You will be spurred on by the desire to have such a handsome plot of your own and to grow such sweet, fresh vegetables. Your neighbour will be a fine source of helpful advice and you can watch covertly out of a window too, if you are too proud to keep on asking. Moreover, traditional vegetable gardening is one of the most straightforward kinds to learn about from a book – and there are plenty of cheap, practical, and clearly illustrated ones readily available.

It will take very little time for you to achieve some success and produce from your plot – which is one of the real bonuses of vegetable gardening for beginners; it takes far, far longer for a good ornamental garden, with trees and shrubs and well-stocked borders, to reach such rewarding maturity. Gardening may be a training in the cultivation of patience as well as of plants, but you need the reward of some quick results to bolster your enthusiasm too, and for this there really is nothing to match the vegetable patch.

But of course you know that gardens are for flowers too. Whether you already have some depends upon the garden you bought. If it was new, you will have a plot which the builders laid to grass, if you were lucky; to mud and empty lager cans if you were not. There will be no trees, shrubs or flowers, and establishing an area for vegetables will so far have taken up all your time and energy. If your garden is a mature one, you will have noticed things emerging and flowering, growing up and dying back as the year moves round. Some you may recognize, others you will not. Should you perhaps be doing anything to or for these things? Perhaps you pick something tentatively or cut back another thing when it spreads across the path and snags your legs as you go by. Perhaps not.

So far, you are only a vegetable grower; gardening in any of its other aspects has not yet got to you. But look over the fence. There is your neighbour's immaculately arranged and thriving plot. You recognize the emerging vegetables readily, you watch him at work, you often chat to him. You have learned a tremendous amount. So you cannot fail to notice that he grows flowers as well as vegetables, bedded out neatly not only in his front garden, but down the long stretch of ground at the back, where he spends all his time. And, in the old-fashioned way, they are alongside and amongst the vegetables. 'Flowers for cutting'; 'flowers for the house'. Sweet peas grow beside the path on a line of canes and string supports, or else, like the runner beans, up a wigwam. There are rows of scabious, that heavenly soft grey-blue, marigolds near the broad beans, sweet williams and asters and, at the end, a row of tidily clipped roses. And the next time a marrow or a cauliflower is handed to you over the fence there is a bunch of flowers as well. They look beautiful on the table in the house and smell marvellous, out of all comparison better than anything the expensive florist can wrap stiffly in cellophane and deliver. If you grew your own, you could have fresh flowers in every room, every day, as well as fresh vegetables in the kitchen.

But how do you grow flowers? Like growing carrots? Ask your neighbour. You vaguely thought that everything came from the local garden centre in pots or, in the case of seeds, from the corner shop. Fine. But your neighbour, the old-fashioned gardener, will probably never *buy* anything at all – and may well never have set foot inside that new-fangled place called the garden centre. He saves his own seed and takes cuttings and pots everything up in his greenhouse.

Ah, the greenhouse. Perhaps you bought one of those along with the house too? It is at the far end, full of cobwebs and dusty little flower pots and an old wooden seed tray or so. You may go in one evening, having just seen your neighbour's astonishing Aladdin's cave of a greenhouse, in which plants climb everywhere and tomatoes smell pungent and benches of seedlings and tiny, delicate-looking flowers are arranged on stages. You pinched the leaf of a scented geranium and carried the curious exotic musky smell home on your fingers and now stand inside your bare, dusty, but suddenly infinitely promising greenhouse and dream dreams and see visions.

The next day you buy some seed compost and begin to fill a few of the little pots, twitching with excitement. You are getting infinite pleasure from the minutiae of growing things. Something has happened to you. You have become one particular sort of gardener.

Those who begin like this, by growing vegetables, begin in the most direct and readily understandable of ways, for the most practical of reasons and by the most straightforward of routes. If you do so, you may be entirely content to continue down that path until your garden looks as good as your neighbour's – which may not take very long; and until you are as good a grower – which will take the rest of your life. It is an enviable and clear-cut beginning. And often the process is subtle, magical and mysterious. You do not feel that you are taking steps to becoming a gardener – rather that something is drawing you on and into the garden, a gentle, irresistible magnetic force.

On the other hand, your garden may simply exist: you pass it on your way in and out of the house, and attend to its more obvious and pressing needs from time to time. You neither like nor dislike it – but merely feel benevolently neutral.

Spring comes. The days lengthen. On one of the first, soft, balmy evenings you smell an astonishing, delicate smell as you walk by the front garden of another neighbour, such a smell as makes you miss a step, stop and go back. There, beside the gate, is a shrub in full flower. What you smelt is both wonderful itself but more, for you much more, for the smell transports you back to childhood and a time you did not remember that you remembered, when you used to spend happy afternoons in the garden of a great aunt. It is not the sight of the shrub that is familiar, only its fragrance and you scarcely know whether you like the look of it. It does not matter. You want that unmistakable, infinitely nostalgic smell close to your own front door so that you can re-visit those days in your imagination again and again.

Now you are on yet another brink. Now, several things may happen as you are pulled gently, irresistibly forward. You may visit a garden centre and find the fragrant shrub. Rather to your dismay, it is quite small though unmistakably the same plant. You buy it and take it home. Now you must either plan carefully where to plant it, which means you begin to look at the whole of your garden with a different and keener eye; or, more likely, you simply find a space near the house so that the shrub will greet you early and late, and bung it in. If it is some hardy old thing, tolerant of any soil or aspect, it will settle down and begin to grow. If not, you will lose it, wonder why and, because the shrub means so much to you, determine to do better next time by finding out what it likes and so, where you went wrong. You discover a book which is most helpful and interesting on the subject of this and other shrubs, and indeed the rest of the garden too. It opens your eyes. You begin to look around you. You may also resort to a book if the longed-for shrub is not in stock at the nursery. Because you have no idea of its name, you will have to identify it so that you can place an order – though most nurserymen are very helpful when trying to satisfy the 'it's pink with pointy leaves and smells unusual' sort of customer.

But if the owner of the shrub is in her garden the next time you go by, things are made both easier and much more delightful and rewarding for you. Not only will she, if she is any sort of a gardener, be more than happy to give you the name of your shrub: she may well begin to tell you about a lot of other things in her garden and so you have found another friend, another treasure house of knowledge and helpful information.

Your interest in the garden has been quickened because of the particular pleasure gained from a single shrub. But now it has every chance of increasing because you like other plants you see and wonder if you have somewhere to put them too. You begin to look deliberately into other people's gardens. And one evening, it is one particular and most delightful garden which affects you profoundly, so that in a flash of pleasure and excitement you understand what it is a garden can do and be to you, how it is rare and special.

Until now you have chatted to your new friend at the front of her house: there seem to be a great many plants here, so that when she talks about 'the garden' you have assumed vaguely that this is what she means and perhaps all that there is. But then, one evening, she invites you to come and 'see the garden' and leads you along the side path and through a closed gate. As you step forwards you stop for a second at your first sight of this enchanted place; here indeed is 'the garden'. As yet, the individual components are a blur. At this moment it is the whole effect which matters, the atmosphere created by everything, plants, trees, shrubs, grass, paths, walls, water, light and shade – minute details of which you are barely aware – all coming together perfectly and harmoniously.

You are given a drink and left to amble about, look at plants, ask a stream of questions, for your new-found friend is like all true gardeners, quite unfazed by your ignorance, more than willing patiently to answer your most elementary questions. You see a dozen plants you love at once and, after a while, begin to notice how certain flowers are grouped, or complement one another as to shape. Your eye is beginning to distinguish and categorize.

But the glory of the garden becomes apparent, not when you are strolling among the beds and borders looking down at individual plants, but when you are sitting in a deckchair in the shade of a wondrously gnarled old pear tree, drink in hand, looking at the reflections in the little pool close by, and wondering where that grassy path that winds out of sight between the rose bushes may possibly lead.

After a while you find out. There is something irresistible about garden paths, they seduce you out of your chair and urge you to follow them. At the end of this one, you find a small, secret glade; here, in January and February you are told, the ground is a mat of snowdrops and aconites, in March of white wood anemones, in May bluebells. Now, there is only a pale-green dappled shade and, beyond, a fence and an old shed with a creamy rose clambering over. 'Look,' your neighbour says. You turn and see, where the glade opens out just to your left, a grey stone wall. In front of the wall is colour – that is what you see, not flowers, not stems and leaves and petals, but simply a block of pure colour, the most heart-stopping, astonishing blue, the blue of a Mediterranean sky or the Aegean Sea in late afternoon, the blue of lapis lazuli, blended with smoky violet. Irises, planted in a broad band along the wall, irises as you have never seen them. The sight arouses not just delight and admiration, it arouses a kind of greed within you. You *want* that colour. Your desire for it is passionate and it startles you, you could not have imagined that such a feeling could be stirred by flowers in a garden. But as you pull yourself away and walk bemusedly back to your chair under the fruit tree, perhaps it dawns on you that you recognize your feelings – you know them well enough. Most people do. You have fallen in love, though not with a person, with a garden.

When you return home, you go at once to look at your own again. What you see is not the same, it disappoints you, of course. But after a few moments, as your eye gets in, superimposed on your very ordinary garden is another; the garden you have just seen begins to emerge out of your own as you stare, like one of those optical illusion pictures in old children's books.

And after all, why not? You see that it is all there, potentially. And so you begin to dream more dreams, see more visions. At first that is all they are and you may well be quite daunted. Where do you begin? To whom do you turn? For now it does not matter. What has happened to you, even if it is not so intense and overwhelming as this, is that you have seen a garden, perhaps the first one, that has spoken to you on a deeper level than ever before. You are on a brink. Desire and ambition will lend you wings like nothing else. The thought of the paradise garden a few yards away may begin to work upon your memory so that, gradually, other moments as intense as the sight of the blue irises rise up and break upon the surface of your consciousness like bubbles. You remember standing in some deep, cool wooded valley as a child, and seeing sheets of primroses at your feet and stretching away all around you, and with the memory of this sight comes a smell too, the damp, strange, slightly mouldy woodland smell which is the faint, sweet scent of the primroses you have picked, pressed up close to your face.

Another garden is there too, very different from your neighbour's but in its own way the same, because it was such a surprise to come upon and gave you the same magical feeling of stepping into another world. You were on holiday and it was hot, too hot, the sun glaring, the shadows of buildings straight and hard and black. Getting slightly lost, you turned a corner and went down a thin side alley and through an open gateway you thought might lead to the delightful hidden restaurant you had read about. It did not. It led you into a garden, an oasis, shady and cool, with raked gravel paths, orange and lemon trees in lines, and small splashy fountains and stone channels of flowing water. You sat on a bench that was perfectly placed in deep shade under a stone arch and the coolth and tranquillity, the green light under the trees, the flowing water and the heady scent of some white climber that cascaded down from the old walls, the whole of it together affected you profoundly; it was rest and refreshment and restoration, like a balm in the heat of the day.

It comes back to you now and you feel as if you were there, not sitting at your kitchen table over a late cup of tea. And your great aunt's garden, brought back to you so vividly by the smell of the flowering shrub that led you to all this – don't you remember other things that were there? A marvellous tree, not like any tree you have seen since – not a beech or an ash or a chestnut – what was it? And some blossom, pale pink on bare branches against the snow. What was that? There were little frilly flowers like carnations that fringed the garden path and smelt of cloves. A currant bush, pungent as cats in the July heat – you remember picking the ripe fruit; and gooseberries too and a strawberry bed. Fruit! Surely, you could have fruit in the beds at the far end of your own garden, now. First thing tomorrow you are going to find out about it.

Having such plans, and the desire to achieve a garden of your own as beautiful and satisfying as that of your neighbour, and the passionate determination to plant a band of blue irises against your own wall at the first possible opportunity, all this will lead you to look long and hard, often critically at what lies beyond your back door. You have begun.

The vision of your own perfect garden will still be hazy in detail. But nevertheless it will lead you on like a star,* becoming clearer through the months ahead, your companion as you go out in search of gardens.

CHAPTER THREE

MR COLLINS INVITED THEM TO TAKE A STROLL IN THE GARDEN, WHICH WAS LARGE AND WELL LAID OUT AND TO THE CULTIVATION OF WHICH HE ATTENDED HIMSELF. TO WORK IN HIS GARDEN WAS ONE OF HIS MOST RESPECTABLE PLEASURES. HERE, LEADING THE PARTY THROUGH EVERY WALK AND CROSS-WALK, AND SCARCELY ALLOWING THEM AN INTERVAL TO UTTER THE PRAISES HE ASKED FOR, EVERY VIEW WAS POINTED OUT WITH A MINUTENESS WHICH LEFT BEAUTY ENTIRELY BEHIND.

JANE AUSTEN
Pride and Prejudice

VISITING

AND IT MAY BEGIN QUITE UNEXPECTEDLY, with a train journey. There are few such useful opportunities to see into so many gardens, one after another and in a very particular way. Your visit to each one is fleeting and your presence detached; most of the usual senses are disengaged and you cannot linger over individual delights. But this becomes a journey of garden comparison and an excellent, intensive way of helping to get your eye in. Your critical faculties will be aroused, not lulled to sleep by heady scents and balmy breezes, sparkling fountains and the prospect of a cream tea. You will find yourself thinking very profitably and productively indeed.

A long train journey is best, one that begins in the heart of a city, snakes slowly out through inner suburbs and outer suburbs, towards detached executive commuter land and beyond, past villages and out into the real country. Each ribbon of terraces and avenues has a slightly different pattern of gardens and things change as you travel from the south to the north of the country.

There are television programmes, books and regular illustrated articles about the British front garden. But it becomes apparent as soon as the train begins to travel out through the suburbs that back gardens are where the main interest lies. In most established streets, terraces and avenues, the front garden is a small square, often behind a rather dull hedge, often with a driveway for cars. There is a handkerchief of lawn and perhaps a shrub border and a hanging basket over the front door or a tub beside it in season. On new estates front gardens are often uniformly landscaped by the developers.

But back gardens tell another story. From a train you see at once how much more they matter. Row after row, like carpets unrolled from outside the kitchen door and running in a strip to the bottom fence, they are laid out for view.

The first essential difference between gardens is very simple and very evident. Some are gardened and some are not.

Some are completely neglected and unkempt. Here, no one cares. Long dismal strips of sparse turf, muddy or worn in patches, peter out into a mess of waist-high nettles at the boundary fence. Sometimes an old car has been abandoned and grubby children are climbing all over it. There may be heaps of rusty iron and an ancient cooker, a motorbike in the process of being dismantled, spewing its entrails on to the cinder path. Here and there are a dilapidated dog kennel, a rotting rabbit hutch, a shed without a door, an empty, mildewed greenhouse with broken panes.

No one tends anything here – though in spring a few daffodils against the fence, established years before by someone else, will come out cheerfully, and the hawthorn hedge always flowers in May, however unregarded.

If it is a warm summer's evening, someone may be in the garden, for the pleasure of simply being in the open air and out of the house, and they will also enjoy the smell of flowers and the shade of a tree belonging to gardens beyond their own.

In between are the gardens of the gardeners, and when you look carefully at a great many of them, you realize very quickly the number of variations upon a garden there are and how every one is in some way an expression of the owner's taste as well as being an indication of what is stocked at the local garden centre.

Some are very bright, a riot of annuals in baskets and beds, window boxes and containers, pink fuchsias and scarlet geraniums and purple petunias massed together. Others feature dwarf conifers and raised beds of ericas. Some will have a patio and a pond; others seem to incorporate every sort of ornament and accessory obtainable – new crazy-paved paths straddled by rustic arches, pools with stone herons standing forever still and gnomes forever fishing, octagonal gazebos and lean-to conservatories, diamond trellis, a stone trellis, birdbaths, tubs, half barrels and ornamental wheelbarrows spilling out petunias.

Gradually your eye begins to distinguish what it does and, even more, does not like. You pick out a well-built stone wall; the proportions seem exactly right to your eye. The train stops for a few moments and you look down upon a calm, green oasis – a line of old apple trees and white lilac leads to a perfectly arrayed vegetable patch; here, pink *Clematis montana* – though you do not yet know its name – has been allowed to clamber over a shed, along a fence, into a tree and so on to curl up the nearest telegraph pole. This appeals to you. The garden featuring all the crazy paving and too many unrelated bits of stone trellis and Japanese-style wooden pergola does not. You begin to ask yourself why. What is it that pleases your eye here and jars on it there? Is it one isolated thing or a combination of ill-assorted elements? Is it the flowers and plants? If so, what is it about them that you do not like? Their colour, shape, the way things are arranged, their relation to the rest of the garden?

For much of the time, of course, you receive only a very general impression of successive gardens as the train speeds by but, as it slows on the approach to a town, your eye will be able to separate some and pick out individual details. Many gardens, it is clear, are a compromise between the needs of a growing family and the stirrings of desire for a real garden. There is a climbing frame, a sandpit or a plastic paddling pool, an old tyre swinging from a tree branch. But there are also vegetables at the end and a flower bed or two close to the house. During the day these gardens will be quiet: only a baby in a pram, a toddler on a swing, someone hanging out washing or a cat on a fence. By early evening, in fine weather, family life will be spilling out from the houses into their gardens and ebbing and flowing around the one who is mowing or clipping, weeding or just pottering about.

There is something particularly pleasing about garden visiting from a train, because it is illicit. You have not been invited in and so much of people's lives is revealed as you peer into their gardens, yet you do not feel that you are snooping, as you do when the train stops and you inadvertently stare straight into a stranger's bedroom. By their very situation the gardens are to some extent on public display, and their owners are proud of them, working in them perhaps, and rather pleased to be showing them off. One or two may even look up from their jobs to wave to you.

And then, twice, the train stops for rather a long time, in that mysterious, unexplained way trains do, and goes very quiet, in a sort of limbo between stations; and each time you look out and find that you are drawn up right beside a garden and can look at it and analyse it carefully. Enjoy it. Or not.

The first is everything a garden should be. Isn't it? There is a lawn, as immaculate as a bowling green, mown in two-tone stripes of vivid green. No dandelion or daisy blemishes its emerald surface and the edges are razor sharp. So are those of the flower beds, two of which are lozenges, exact as stencils cut out of the turf. Within the beds are tulips, arranged in blocks of colour like snooker balls set out at the start of a match. To one side of the lawn is regularly laid stone paving; to the other a border in which a great deal of meticulously weeded soil is visible beneath the immaculately ordered floribunda roses. What ornament the garden has is neat: a square, concrete birdbath and a line of trellis fencing severing the flower from the vegetable garden, which is as tidily laid out as a canteen of cutlery. Everything is tidy here, everything clipped and mown. And all flowering brightly at its best. The standard of the horticulture is first class. This is a garden. No one tinkers with motors here, no children strew sand and little tricycles.

You are impressed. No? No, oddly depressed, though puzzled as to why. You are faintly repelled by the rigid order which a human hand has imposed upon growth and must surely keep on imposing, day after day, without let-up, alert for every weed, every leaf out of place or petal shed.

The train stirs, shudders and begins to move again and, as it does so, the owner of the garden comes from the shed pulling a flying mower on the end of a long electric lead and begins to mow, lawn proud, as if he wielded an outdoor vacuum cleaner. And after it will come the shears and the clippers and the edging tool. Blades are this man's pride,* clean, bright, oiled and sharpened; with them he has cowed his garden into submission.

The train glides away. You will never see his garden again and are glad of that, though you feel obscurely guilty to recoil in this way from a garden typical of half the gardens of England. And for a while slump back in your seat, finish off your book, turning away from the window. Perhaps you do not like gardens after all, perhaps you can never be a gardener.

You are on another brink. Until the train, already overdue, stops again, sighs and settles down, ticks a little.

It is quite a while before, disillusioned as you have become with this enforced visiting of gardens you do not like, you look crossly out of the window. And see a garden you like very much indeed, an astonishing garden, a garden you could never have conceived of. It is not so much beautiful, shady and delightful, glowing, luxuriant – though, as you stare and stare you see that it is all of these things and more besides. But no. It is a garden of the purest fantasy, an eccentric garden. A garden that makes you smile. You want to get out of the window and walk out of the train and walk into it and around it, feel yourself welcomed and enfolded in a delightful and light-hearted garden embrace.

It is a garden of sweet disorder. At first it looks a tangled mass of plants climbing, plants rambling, plants running riot. But the chaos falls into place as you look into it and you see a certain purpose and evidence of a gently controlling hand. Some gardens have statuary, very old and grand, or else very raw and new: this garden has an old headstone, swathed in ivy, and a battered grieving angel, around which tendrils of clematis are wound. From the deep grass old chimney pots emerge, planted with anything, parsley, strawberries, daisies: there is an ancient railway sign and a signal forever pointing up to go and a path made from old patterned tiles and pieces of broken china. Cabbages intermingle with flowers. Ancient galvanized buckets painted bright blue and green line the steps and make do as flower tubs. There are tiny little pink and blue flowers in old seed pans and troughs scattered everywhere.

Nothing looks planned and yet this is no jungle: the nettles and thistles and cow parsley that are thick towards the boundary fence have not been allowed to encroach further. There is a vegetable patch, well tilled and apparently full only of marrow plants and, along the roof of an old corrugated lean-to at the side of the house, a vine grows in great swags.

Looking into a garden like this, except *there is* no garden 'like this' – you look at the revelation of a personality, you feel you know the owners and their way of life, know them and would like them. Not everything here is to your taste. You would not want an old privy with the door off and the pan sprouting pink geraniums. But the charms of the garden and the dottiness of its character have delighted you – and more than delighted: you have taken a step forwards, because you had been made to see that a garden can be more than a home for plants and a space for growing produce: it can be the expression of a personality, it can please and tease and intrigue.

You have seen dull gardens, ugly gardens, cowed gardens and you will see a very great many other kinds when you go garden visiting from now on – pompous self-important gardens, romantic gardens, dowdy and pretty and peculiar gardens.

But as the train begins to move again, you look back and go on looking regretfully, as if this little garden tucked in below the railway track were a much-loved friend being left behind on a platform. For this is the first garden which has transformed your mood entirely, cheered you up and made you happy. Some gardens you never forget. Particularly not such rare and precious ones, the gardens that make you smile.

PERHAPS THIS INVOLUNTARY, passive garden visiting has whetted your appetite for the real thing. Your gardening friends offer advice on the best local gardens to visit. An advertisement in the local garden centre catches your eye: 'Garden Open for the Red Cross. Plant stall.' The last phrase makes you wonder; do gardeners really take their plants for walks and stall them while they walk round the garden? Someone mentions a Yellow Book, which seems to be the garden visitors' bible; really serious individuals have two, one in the car and one in the house. You buy a copy – remarkably cheap!

A new world opens up. You had no idea so many private gardens welcomed visitors – and some all the year round. Here, gardens a hundred feet by thirty rub shoulders with famous parks of a hundred acres 'laid out by Capability Brown', gazebos, ten-acre woodland gardens, parterres, laburnum walks, lakes, cascades, waterfalls and fountains;

gardens specializing in one kind of plant, national collections of shrubs and trees; chains of gardens in the same road or the same village opening on the same day; gardens that have been featured (as they say) on television; established gardens claiming descent from Gertrude Jekyll, and some only two or three years old – that is encouraging. The choice is overwhelming, but there must be something here to give you ideas for your own garden. Some are open on several days but some only on one; you make a note in your diary.

A visit to a garden open under the National Gardens Scheme is always a gamble. The brief description in the Yellow Book may conceal great beauties or it may inflate a visitor's expectations. What does 'owner-maintained' mean and why should the owner include it in the description of the garden? Is the owner a full-time gardener or a busy executive who has little time to maintain his plot? Is it an excuse for neglect and to what standard is the garden maintained? People have quite different ideas of maintenance; some love a garden that has little apparent tending, where herbaceous borders are bursting with plants growing into each other and out over the path; some love the sight of neatly hoed earth and precisely pruned roses. 'Plants for sale' may mean a few scraggy specimens in weed-infested pots, or a small, immaculately kept nursery of rarities. Almost all gardens claim to grow 'unusual plants'; what does this mean? Can we really expect to find things that are unique in each of these gardens, or only plants that the owners think we do not grow in our own gardens? How many people must grow a plant before it ceases to be unusual? Beth Chatto's plants were unusual when she began her nursery, but so successful has she been in persuading us all of their beauty that the term is now a cliché. Increasingly, we find an entry that reads 'small arboretum newly planted'; this may mean five acres of 'unusual' trees, well labelled, or a corner in which five new trees huddle too close together in a tangle of unkempt grass.

But there is no better way of learning what pleases you than to visit such gardens: the owner is often on hand with practical advice on how to grow the plants that you admire. If the garden is near your own, the advice will be of special relevance. Talking to the garden's maker will expand the visitor's stock of ideas on which to draw in making his own place. Thus, he will perhaps start to question assumptions which are rooted so deeply they are not even recognized as assumptions at all; for example, most people in this country assume a garden must have a lawn. Then they will visit a garden where there is no lawn; the owner thinks grass is monotonous and requires too much work in its upkeep. Yes, one visitor admits, ruefully thinking of the hours spent obediently following the mower up and down the mandatory stripes. Another's reaction may be different; now I see why my lawn gives so much pleasure. It is an oasis of peace among the hectic planting and, when newly mown – delighting the nostrils – shadows cast on it look so clean cut. Whatever the reaction, an assumption has been questioned and the principles that form taste have been developed.

When we visit gardens with our eyes open, we will be constantly questioning. This can't be done when the major purpose of the visit is to take the family on an outing; only when there is leisure to linger over a planting, or to consider why an effect of light or shade is so successful, or how the designer has dealt with such an awkwardly shaped site. This is a different kind of garden visiting, and it is best done alone or with a like-minded friend. An essential piece of equipment on such a visit is the notebook in which to jot down names of exciting, unfamiliar plants, design details and other information gleaned from the owner, such as the address of her favourite nursery.

There are as many ways of assessing the success of a particular garden as there are visitors. And we must always remember that our assessment is based only on how we saw the garden at that particular moment; our judgement will be influenced by the season, the time of day, the weather and, like all critics, by the state of our digestion. A garden in Galicia had seemed particularly beautiful on a sunny summer evening. Six months later, a visitor to whom it had been recommended complained that it bore almost no resemblance to the garden as described. What had happened? In such a moist climate plants grow very fast so, if maintenance is not constant, the jungle can easily take over; perhaps this is what had happened. Or was Santiago de Compostela living up to its nickname – *el orinal d'España* (the chamberpot of Spain), so that her visit to the neighbouring garden was cold and damp? Or perhaps her critical reaction was simply the result of a bad lunch.

Visiting the garden of a great home, particularly a National Trust garden, is something different. A visit to Sissinghurst in Kent or to Hidcote is a search for a standard by which to assess other gardens and perhaps our own. You want to see what the best is like; the best care of plants, the best colour compositions, the best examples of a particular species, the best proportions, the best-made steps and paths, the best use of water, and so on. Most visitors will not be able to attain quite the effect they admire but will carry home a dreamily satisfied impression of beauty, and perhaps a few ideas which can be tried out at home; even if they do not work, they will serve to recall the glories of the ideal garden. And, of course, such gardens make excellent objectives for a drive and settings for a day out.

As the novice gardener begins to develop a taste, certain questions will recur on each garden visit. Great gardens, like any great work of art, manage to combine a sense of order and repose with excitement. The sense of order is achieved by the firm statement of themes in the garden; for example, the rooms at Hidcote or the rigid layout of brick walls, yew hedges and walks at Sissinghurst. But within this structure there will be the variety that impels the excited visitor from one space to the next; at Hidcote, for example, we move from an elegant, continental, stilt garden with its raised boxes of hornbeam and almost no colour, down some steps to find a red garden, glowing with exotic plants. At Sissinghurst in high summer the bright colours of the planting in the cottage garden are a shock after the restrained tones elsewhere.

Someone looking with a critical eye will also notice how enclosed different parts of the garden are and, if they are clearly defined, what the boundaries are made of. Some gardens are a series of tightly enclosed spaces, so that the visitor moves as through a maze, never knowing the whole garden but only seeing what is allowed of the next space. Other kinds of enclosure allow the eye to travel where the feet cannot, so we can appreciate the pattern of the whole, but must explore the space in a regulated fashion. This is achieved on a small scale in the currently fashionable 'potager' vegetable garden, where the pattern of box edging gives unity to the design, while the visitor must walk along the straight paths. On a different scale, we see the same effect in the use of the ha-ha and in the landscape designs of Brown or Repton, where the carriage drive sweeps through the park with glimpses of the house between trees and hills, so that the arrival at the grand entrance is full of drama. Such glimpses of an objective can be contrived in various ways. Low hedges, like the box edging in the potager, will have this effect, or high hedges with crenellated tops, or portholes which invite us to peer through. Or the material used to define the enclosure may be light, like trellis, so that we are both enclosed by it and yet can see beyond it if we are determined enough. A row of trees can mark a boundary; the space in between them will regulate the sense of freedom or enclosure.

Different parts of the garden may be treated in different ways; some parts will be made to walk through, others to sit or spend time in. The proportions of the space will create the mood – for example, tall hedges planted close together will create the feeling of a corridor, so that we will want to move through that area, while larger but still defined open spaces will be tranquil and invite repose. Gardens that grow bit by bit, with no overall plan or design, can sometimes have a feeling of restlessness because they have no centre; the visitor is constantly on the move and never gets the feeling of having arrived at the heart of the garden. An excess of excitement can leave us as unsatisfied as lack of mystery.

Of course, enclosing a space is only one way of defining it. Changing the material underfoot can change the feeling – walking on grass, say, after walking on stone paving. And a change of mood can be achieved by a change in the way the planting is handled; at its simplest level, this can be a change from close-mown grass to rough grass or, most conventionally, the remoter parts of the garden may be dominated by shrubs and trees, while closer to the house there are herbaceous borders and alpines. Another part of the garden may define itself around a fountain or a piece of sculpture.

Thus, the visitor's attention will move from the structure of the garden to its details – the patterns of colour; patterns of texture; the use of water, statuary and so on. Ideas gleaned from these details will fill the notebook, particularly ideas about successful combinations of colour, because these can be tried out in a garden of any size. It is possible to work out theories of colour and to follow them in the planting of a whole border. At The Priory in Kemerton, Peter and Elizabeth Healing did just that, and their great border, a hundred and fifty feet long and eighteen feet deep, must be among the most superb in the country, particularly in August when many gardens are beginning to look tired. The colours start from the palest greys, warm up with creams, pinks and pale yellows, reach blood heat with purples and violets, boiling point with oranges and scarlets, then simmer down through a similar range of colours to whites and greys at the far end. Not content with this excitement, they then planted a scarlet border that is breathtaking.

Then there are the focal points; these may be statuary, old tubs, seats, terracotta pots – whatever draws the eye, thus giving a focus to a space. Are they well situated, are they appropriate and in proportion to the surroundings? Seats serve two functions – to be looked at and to be looked from. Some seats are beautiful but not at all comfortable, and vice versa, so it is necessary to decide which function is the more important. It's also important to think about the placing of a seat. In a fine Portuguese garden at the Palace of Queluz, just outside Lisbon, the seats are placed where there is no view at all, presumably because, like the whole garden, they were intended for the introverted social activity of the Court, not for solitary contemplation. It is also worth thinking about any water features used as focal points; how fountains and water spouts are placed and what effect they have. Is the water creating a mood of excitement or one of peace?

Finally, how well does the garden complement the house? A grand house like Blickling, in Norfolk, is splendidly complemented by the giant parterre with its enormous square beds and long borders, designed in 1933 by Nancy Lindsay to take the place of a more elaborate scheme of beds which became impossible to maintain. Tintinhull, in Somerset, gives us an idea of what can be done on a much smaller scale. Here the traditional pattern of a formal garden near the house, more informal further away, has been adapted with great subtlety. From the drawing-room door we look down a straight path, defined by a line of box cut into symmetrical domes, which runs through three kinds of garden – the first enclosed by a high wall, the next an informally planted space, defined by a great evergreen oak (*Quercus ilex*), and finally, a formally patterned white garden with a fountain in the middle; this has drawn our eyes and our feet since it was first seen sparkling against a background of yew.

Just beyond the fountain there is a seat, beautifully placed so that we can enjoy the reverse view along the path to the west front of the house. Each of these three spaces is in perfect proportion to the lovely, classical façade. And from the second and third spaces, openings allow access to larger gardens with less restrained plantings. The area of the flower garden at Tintinhull is scarcely one acre, but it feels much larger because the different spaces are treated in such varied ways. Yet all is harmonious with the fine and unpretentious house.

But the garden at Tintinhull turns its back on the countryside. The rolling fields and big skies of this part of Somerset would have dwarfed a garden that had to be small in scale, to suit the house. It is possible to achieve a similar range of effects, even in a comparatively small city garden.

For many, garden visiting may be an end in itself, one of the delightful pleasures of life. Those without gardens of their own can enjoy other people's for a day; for them, there is the added charm born of the realization that, when confronted by a bed in need of weeding or a high hedge to be clipped, these are entirely someone else's responsibility.

The pleasure of planning a garden visiting day is considerable too – poring over the Yellow Book and *The Good Gardens Guide* and route maps, working out the most attractive way of getting there and, if there is a choice, the best time of day to arrive.

The retired in particular, whose interest in gardens and gardening is often at its peak, can enjoy visits on week days and outside school and public holidays, when all but a handful of the most popular gardens will be far less crowded. In the early morning and at the end of the afternoon, it is perfectly possible to have whole gardens, especially lesser-known ones and those off the beaten track, entirely to oneself.

A day out, a happy few hours spent ambling round a good garden, tea with home-made cakes and then home. There are few more straight-forward, innocent and happy pleasures to be had. And that may be all.

The pleasure can be spun out, of course, and intensified and elaborated, after the visit itself is over: in talking about the garden seen, on the way back and, depending on how interesting – and perhaps controversial – it has been, for days afterwards. Those who like to take photographs will have the added bonus of getting them back, using them as reminders and arranging them on bleak days of the following winter.

But there may be even more, and gardens may be reflected upon to some purpose. To begin with, the memory of the day will be a confusion and the recollection of the garden itself be overlaid with surface impressions and detail of what happened: the fact that there was a downpour in the middle of the afternoon; the irritating, chattering coachload of guided visitors who seemed not to know why they were there at all; the small child rescued in the nick of time from the edge of a steep ha-ha; getting lost on the way home – *and whose fault was that?* But gradually the memories of the day are shaken down, irrelevancies sifted and forgotten, and then the garden itself emerges and is revealed, whole and clear again in the mind's eye, to be revisited, walked around, studied again and again, quietly, slowly. And it is then, for those who do want to take the process further, that the best lessons of garden visiting begin to be learnt.

First, there is the impression you gained of the whole garden – that almost instinctive, first and complete response that is perhaps the most important of all. 'I liked it . . . I didn't much care for it . . . That was wonderful: the most beautiful garden I have ever seen.' Not every garden will provoke such a complete response – often it will be a question of 'liking in part' – and occasionally a garden will be so bland and dull that it will have provoked scarcely any response at all and so be instantly forgotten.

Once the whole garden has been looked at again, clear and whole in the mind, the details will begin to emerge: you can recall a border, a particular grouping of plants, one shrub, one tree; the pattern of a well-laid brick path, shadows thrown on to the grass by the pillars of a pergola, a collection of pots on a step, the particular way gravel was raked. What did you like? You can tell. You can begin to work out exactly why.

A visit to any fine garden cannot fail to stimulate ideas about what might be done in one's own. Of course there will be many things no one could or should imitate, and in any case slavish copying is no more a good idea in garden planning than in other areas of life. But noticing how well something works in a good garden never fails to be helpful, though detail will necessarily be modified in translation.

When you are on the threshold of gardening, it is easy to admire, to be impressed and overawed; and to be daunted, too, by the glories of a fine, well-planned and mature garden. But at least you can feel confident that this response is the one you ought to be having, just as the aspiring poet or painter will naturally expect to be overwhelmed by the work of any great master.

No, it is the other sort of response which is the problem. You visited a garden – perhaps it was a modest garden nearby, open on just one Sunday afternoon for charity. You spent an hour there; so did a lot of other people who all seemed very appreciative. You met the owners who seemed very proud indeed. But *you* did not like the garden at all. You keep quiet about that because you are a complete beginner and surely all those experienced and admiring visitors cannot be wrong? The owners have spent years of their life, hour after hour, with bent backs or on their knees, making their garden grow. They know more about plants and how to make them thrive than you will probably ever learn in your lifetime, so how dare you come along at this stage in your garden career and think, 'I don't like it'!

Even worse, you drive fifty miles to see a garden designed by someone with a very grand and famous name, which you have been told is not just a good garden but an *important* garden.

You hate it. There is almost nothing about its layout, its design, the plants and trees and shrubs and hedges and vegetables that you like. Surely this cannot be right.

For the rest of the season of garden visiting you see a lot that seems beautiful or striking, plants you would love to grow, details of garden design you admire and would love to translate, somehow, into the garden you plan for yourself. But quite often, too, you see things you dislike very much indeed, and which you would rigorously exclude. And still, you keep quiet and for a long time dare not admit your extremes of taste, even to yourself.

But if, as someone said, 'Taste is made up of a thousand small distastes', you will one day be forced to acknowledge that you have many strong dislikes in the garden and at that point you will ask, 'Does it matter?'

Surely not.

Reaching that conclusion is a great moment, a watershed. It is the first important step towards. . . .

CHAPTER FOUR

THERE ARE NO MYSTERIOUS 'MUSTS', NO SET RULES, NO FINGER OF SHAME POINTED AT THE GARDENER WHO DOESN'T FOLLOW AN ACCEPTED PATTERN.
LANDSCAPING IS NOT A COMPLEX AND DIFFICULT ART TO BE PRACTISED ONLY BY HIGH PRIESTS.

Thomas D. Church
Gardens Are for People

LIBERATION

S O YOU HAVE A GARDEN. You want to tend it and make it look good: you have seen many that you very much like when out garden visiting and in photographs too, and they have inspired you. You are gradually discovering plants you like and want to grow yourself and learning more about them, from other gardeners and from books and catalogues and what is on display at the nursery. Your tastes are forming, your interest is growing and the excitement of it all is beginning to get to you. You are on the verge of becoming a serious gardener. But at this early and vulnerable stage, quite a few things may cause you to falter in your stride.

You had never expected gardening to be an armchair activity – and indeed, some of the work in prospect is positively appealing: you like the idea of pottering in a greenhouse, working in the peace, warmth and quiet with plants, handling them tenderly, taking a pride in the first, frail shoots you have nurtured. The idea of being outdoors a lot is pleasing too, and in certain moods you feel sure you will derive a great deal of satisfaction from grubbing out a hedge bottom, making a flower bed completely weed free or plodding rhythmically up and down the lawn behind the mower. But looking around you in the spring and summer, you note that gardens are like hives of worker bees – a person busy doing something in every one, every available daylight hour. Even on fine, warm summer evenings, when you feel the garden is there to be sat in, admired and enjoyed over a long, slow drink, you fear you are in a minority of one: everyone else seems to be hoeing, clipping, or tying back, and the peace of those blissful Sunday afternoons you had looked forward to, asleep after lunch in your deckchair, is fractured by the whirr and whine of a thousand garden machines.

Then there are all those 'jobs for the week' articles in the newspapers, which reinforce your impression that gardening is a never-ending chore, as they bossily remind you that you should already have begun to mulch/prune/spray/fork over. It is easy to become dispirited at the prospect of all this. Gardening has traditionally been presented as what the writer Ursula Buchan so aptly describes as 'the outdoor equivalent of DIY'.

Indeed, you have already noted that the indoor areas of many garden centres arrange their stock in that regimented way reminiscent of the DIY superstores – which generally do have a gardening department indistinguishable, in its neatly stacked rows of tools and packets of weed killer and fertilizers, from the home decorating or plumbing sections. A visit to either is not calculated to lift the spirits or excite the imagination.

Only look, in February and March, at the miles of display shelving devoted to the lawn: products with which, apparently, you must feed it, poison selected bits of it, aerate it, rake it, spray it, water it and trim its edges neatly – as well, of course, as mowing it twice a week without fail. Confronted by the means to accomplish all these tasks, you wonder despairingly whether you can't just have a patch of grass?

The answer, of course, is yes. Yes, yes, and more yes. You need do none of these things to your grass except mow it, and even that, like haircutting, need not be performed so frequently or vigorously as nanny would have led you to believe. You can even get away, in the orchard or some wild-flower areas, with scarcely ever cutting your grass at all. If you really rather like having daisies and speedwell on your lawn and are happy to put up with a little seasonal shagginess about the edges, you will save yourself a great deal of work and worry* and you can safely leave the lawn section to those whose chief gardening aim is to own a velvety emerald sward of bowling-green flatness.

Alternatively, you can do away with grass altogether and go in for raked gravel, say, or York stone flags – though you do need to think very carefully about these and should probably take some expert advice before committing yourself; they are expensive and can bring a few maintenance problems of their own along with them. But whatever you choose to do, you *can* be released from the tyranny of the lawn; and the moment you realize this may be your first moment of garden liberation.

It is not only inessential jobs you need to be free of – it is general garden guilt. For it is not at all difficult to be made to feel vaguely guilty about gardening, however enthusiastic you are, however much work you do. Indeed, garden work makes more garden work, it is self-perpetuating and, strive as hard as you can, you will never liberate yourself in that way. You will be like Alice in Looking-Glass country, where she had to run as hard and fast as she could just to stay in the same place. To be liberated from garden guilt, while at the same time still enjoying a garden, requires a rather more sideways approach.

If you have begun your gardening life with a vegetable patch, several species and sub-species of guilt will have found a rich soil in which to flourish. But such guilt often has soft, sappy roots and is quite easily eradicated, though you will always have to be on your guard against the appearance of a seedling or two, and have it up promptly before it can take hold.

When you look around you at some allotments, or at the kitchen gardens of your neighbours, you may see immaculate rows of cabbages, cauliflowers and carrots, beans and peas, potatoes and lettuces, onions and broccoli, leeks, kale, parsnips, turnips, marrows – not to mention greenhouses stuffed to bursting with tomatoes and cucumbers and even, in a few ambitious instances, exotica like aubergines and peppers. Daunting? Yes. You wonder if you will ever cope with the demands of such a vegetable garden and it is true that vegetables need attention – lots of it at various stages – and that some of the work among them can be heavy and dull. But you certainly want to eat your own produce, so you suppose, a little wearily, that you had simply better get stuck in and retire as secretary of the tennis club and from the amateur dramatics society and the darts team, too, on the grounds of lack of time. Wait a moment. Even if you want to be a gardener, there is no law that says you have to grow any vegetables at all. Just because you have the ground doesn't mean it has to be filled with cabbages. You can grow lilies instead. Or make a raised bed for alpines. Or have a wildlife pond where the kitchen garden might have been.

But if you *do* grow vegetables, it ought to be self-evident that you are perfectly free to grow only the ones you actually enjoy eating,* and those which are best picked absolutely fresh and plopped at once into the cooking pan – new potatoes or tiny broad beans. You can buy perfectly good onions or swede in a shop and they are rarely expensive. Growing your own is scarcely worthwhile; they are quite a lot of trouble and they take up too much space. And really, an onion is an onion, and you won't be able to taste the difference between home-grown and shop-bought beetroot – if beetroot is the sort of thing you like.

The moment these things are written down they seem so obvious, yet it is surprising how many people go on year after year growing vegetables they do not like and then desperately trying to bribe friends to take them away, especially when there is a glut; and nature is remarkably good at making up for things – if it's a bad year for carrots you can be sure it will be a bumper one for sprouts. There always is a glut of something (though very rarely of the things you can never have too much of, like asparagus).

So more moments of liberation come when it dawns on you that you do not have to grow any vegetable you don't actually like,* or need to have absolutely fresh, or find difficult in your particular soil, or too time-consuming; and when you also realize that your kitchen garden is not required by law to be enormous. People often have the vague idea that vegetables require a great deal of space – they think of allotments or the two-acre kitchen garden on that television programme. But of course you can have just as much or as little space devoted to vegetables as you choose. Perhaps it is all a hangover from wartime and 'Digging for Victory', coupled with some vaguely 'green' notions – if you are privileged enough to have land, you feel you ought to make full use of it, and if a family, ergo, you must feed it, especially when half the world is starving. Noble sentiments. Are you really going to ship your surplus produce to the Third World? Are you aware that most children loathe most vegetables? Will you be content when the reward for hours of backbreaking work is a glut of leeks as appetizing as tentpoles?

You can be free of all this; free to grow only tiny new potatoes or a whole acre of broad beans; free to have just an asparagus bed, or vegetables in the herbaceous border, or a couple of raised beds two feet square with tiny rows of a few vegetables to be picked very young, or a single handsome wigwam of runner beans lording it over the roses. It's a fine moment when you decide unilaterally never to give garden room to any radish.

Vegetable gardening ought to be all pleasure: pleasure in the dark-brown fine tilth in which you sow the seeds or plant things out, pleasure in the vivid green and squeakiness of fresh cabbage or spinach leaves; pleasure in eating peas, pod and all, as you pick them, pleasure in the smell of pinched-off tomato shoots and the wonderful earthiness of newly dug potatoes. Pleasure in taking indoors and cooking and eating, eating, eating.

Pleasure may be obtained in other quite arcane and unexpected ways too, as John Carey, Oxford don and prize vegetable grower, so wonderfully describes.

> With the best will in the world, it's difficult to pretend that the parsnip is really eatable, but it's an immense and exacting pleasure to grow. At the start of the season, you grub out a row of pits with a trowel and fill them almost to the brim with finely sieved soil. Then you poke into each soft dell about a dozen of the crisp wafers which are the parsnip seeds and pat earth over them. Come the summer, you pull out all but one of the seedlings from each cluster – pale gold pencils with feathery tops, which it always gives you a pang to throw onto the compost heap, though there's nothing else to be done with them. Then, as the winter approaches, the great spreading leaves of the survivors rot, and yellow, and the parsnips withdraw into their subterranean existence until, sometime after Christmas, the time comes to crack the frosty crust over them and lug them out, gross, whiskered and reeking from their lairs.

The Green movement has successfully added to the potential load of guilt borne by gardeners, and the beginner may well arrive with some of it already weighing heavy upon his shoulders. Spraying anything with anything is apparently forbidden, nor are you allowed to nourish your growing plants with a nice feed of something nitrogenous; the word 'chemical' is politically incorrect and has everywhere been replaced by 'organic'. It is all very intimidating. Some of the decisions have already been made for the gardener – certain poisons and pesticides, for example, are no longer commercially available. Otherwise the matter is, and should remain, one of personal choice. To be wholly green, moderately green, or not green at all – it is entirely up to you to decide.

Nor do you have to be tyrannized by the taste of the garden snobs, those who would have you believe that fashions in garden design, ornament or plants matter one jot. There are class divisions in gardening as in everything else, but you need not join any of the ghettos; there are those who care about such things and grow for show, to keep up appearances, to make style statements; those for whom it very much matters to have the right, and never the wrong, plants. Fine. That is their privilege and their pleasure. Garden snobbery is harmless enough so long as it is of the aspiring and not the sneering variety.

Liberation comes when you read the 'in' gardening writers, look at their plans, see photographs of their gardens, and can decide whether or not you like any of them entirely on merit and appeal; when you do not worry whether variegated plants and bedded-out petunias are common or gnomes fishing in pools a mark of lower-class tastes. You like gnomes? Have them. You want a garden modelled on the principles of Vita Sackville-West? Good luck to you. You can still keep an open mind, change your likes and dislikes over the years, learn from the best and avoid or overcome expensive or ugly mistakes. *It's your garden*.

This absolute rule – that you can have in it exactly what you choose – applies as much to flowers and shrubs as to vegetables. Reading books, looking at gardens, visiting garden centres, watching or listening to programmes may make your heart sink because there seems to be so much you have to have in the garden. Have to? Just because God made euphorbias, you do not have to grow them. There may be very many plants you greatly dislike – ericas, bright tulips, anything scarlet or spotted, fuchsias, little box hedges, old roses, wisteria, dahlias, all those obscure little brown plants which are difficult to grow – the list is endless. You are ashamed to admit that they don't please you. But why ever should you be? If you want to hate cotoneaster, go ahead and hate it. If it is already in your garden, have it out.

Oh, yes – you are allowed to do that too. There is a particularly nasty form of garden guilt which strikes when you so much as toy with the idea of uprooting something, not because it is dead or diseased – that seems to be allowed, though only after all attempts at resuscitation have failed – but simply because you hate it, or it does not look right where it is. You may well have been led to believe that if it grows it is sacred and untouchable – the horticultural equivalent of 'if it is printed and between hard covers it is called a book and great guilt will attach to its wanton destruction'. Rubbish. If you loathe that *Garrya elliptica*, get rid of it. If you think clematis would look much prettier climbing over the fence than purple wisteria, get one out and the other in. There is no shortage of plants in the world and for every gardener who loathes begonias there will be ten who love them.

If you want to have no flowers in your garden save blue ones, do; if you are someone who only likes roses, only grow roses – or at least begin that way. After a time you may find that roses are set off to perfection if one or two other plants are allowed to soften their unattractively naked lower stems – nepeta, say, or lavender – and that some look particularly fine grown against a background of dark, glossy evergreens. You find yourself becoming interested in those and even liking them for themselves and so your gardening taste may develop. Your first and best love will still be the roses, for some years at least (after which time you may even rebel against them completely, like the eccentric gardening guru Christopher Lloyd, who in vigorous old age has become violently anti-rose).

You may like to look at a completely bare garden in winter, preferably through a window. You will be accused of being a fair-weather gardener, of course, not a proper one at all. 'Proper gardeners' have Something of Colour and Interest All the Year Round, rush out to count how many plants are blooming on 1 January, and spend part of every single day doing something in the garden, no matter what the elements have to hurl at them. But it is perfectly possible to put your garden to bed at the end of October and not step into it again until March – possible and in no way reprehensible – though of course there is much pleasure to be had from strolling round on one of those astonishingly mild, sunny days we always do get in February and discovering that the place is full of hellebores, winter aconites and snowdrops, with crocuses just starting to push through. And the pleasure of bulbs is enhanced by knowing that you don't have to do anything to them once they are established, except add more.

Like Christopher Lloyd, have the courage of your convictions. But remember, you *may* one day see a variegated shrub or a red flower or an erica that you actually like. At first you will like it but only in someone else's garden. You may or may not reach the stage of wanting to have it in your own. After that, who knows, you may one day hold the National Collection.

Gardens should be places of delight and pleasure, refreshment and solace, inspiration and glory. Your garden is yours. Your retreat, your pleasure, your reward for hard labour. Yours. Within its bounds you are free. Gardens should not mean drudgery and putting up with what you do not like – other people's taste, second best. There is no gardener more contented and satisfied, no gardener happier than the Liberated Gardener.

CHAPTER FIVE

As a rule a French garden, in the style of Louis XIV, is a drawing room or gallery in the open air, a place to stroll and converse in company. In an English garden, the kind they have invented and propagated, one is better alone, so that the eyes and the soul can converse with nature.

Hippolyte Taine
Notes on England

DRAMA

Visiting a garden can be more like reading a novel than looking at a picture. We are hooked by the first chapter but not satisfied by it. When we arrive in a garden it must give us a sense that we have entered a new world with a character and definition of its own. But it is not enough that we have arrived – there must also be the temptation to explore further. Paths curving out of sight, gateways, gaps in hedges, the sound of falling water, will each impel us to discover what delights lie in store. A guide is not needed: the gardens themselves tell us which way to go. They tempt and tease the visitor and thus impress themselves on the memory; these are the enchanted places.

There must be tension to lure us on, but not too much tension. Like all works of art, gardens must provide both excitement and repose, the one contrasting with the other and so highlighting it. We may not readily think of tension in relation to gardens, yet it is not difficult to think of those that are merely drab, that at first sight seem perfect but ultimately leave us unsatisfied. These are the gardens where there is a lack of drama and where everything is in such uniform 'good taste' that it is easy to predict what will come next. All colour tones are muted, no risks have been taken, no personality allowed to show through. Good gardens will be peaceful, but if the sense of peace becomes monotonous, it will swiftly be replaced by boredom. There can be great drama in the use of colour and, indeed, colours can be combined with all the tension and conflict of the boldest melodrama. But too often these jazzy mixtures are used again and again: how much more interesting if they were contrasted with calmer colours elsewhere – as they are at Sissinghurst, where the brilliant oranges and scarlets in the cottage garden are so much more exciting by contrast with the quieter tones in other places.

But there is another kind of drama which comes from the treatment of space (though it need not assume that the garden is immense, as did the Victorian lecturer whose section on woodland began: 'However small your garden, at least an acre should be devoted to trees.'). Even a very small one can have different areas, conveying different moods: they may be defined by light and shade and by the surfaces underfoot – grass or gravel, brick or stone; by planting in bright or subdued colours; by boundaries, of hedge or fence or espaliered trees. They can be divided into areas for different functions, too – one for the children with sandpits and a bit of jungle for dens near a mature tree, which might be ideal for a treehouse, and an open space, seeded with tougher grass, for football and cricket. There may be a separate area for sitting, sheltered from the wind, given the special pleasure of a concentration of scented flowers and shrubs, and perhaps even a place for sunbathing, but with a shade tree close by.

A sense of drama is achieved in many gardens by open spaces which lead into some kind of enclosure: any garden is better for having a place to be private in, somewhere secluded – a kind of paradise in its original sense. (The English word is a transliteration of the Persian *pairidaeza*, which literally means a place that is walled around.) This particular kind of paradise is a space that is just one person big, a retreat for times when convoluted problems need sorting out, a haven from intrusive demands and in which to recall Marvell's lines, 'Two paradises 'twere in one/To live in paradise alone.' Such a misanthropic mood may not strike often, but when it does a garden, just as much as a house, should provide a space in which to indulge it. At other times, this single space may be for dreaming, for gathering together the sundered parts of oneself, or simply for gathering wool – a most valuable pastime. This sanctuary, which is really no more than the adult version of the child's den, may be a seat with a view, a bank in a warm corner, or a bower beneath a trellis canopy where climbing roses and honeysuckle scent the air. It could be a tiny island in the middle of a pool, reached by a one-person boat, or a modest tree house (with rope ladder to pull up behind one), gazebo, or other eyrie, down among trees and shrubs at the bottom of the garden, with some view out yet screened from the rest of the world. The essence of these private places is that they are small, enclosed and secluded.

If you are thinking bigger thoughts, then your private place may become a secret garden. In medieval times this was called the *hortus conclusus*; here, noble ladies did their embroidery, noble lads read their verses, monks elevated their thoughts, and any of the above might give way to dalliance which could, as in Chaucer's 'The Merchant's Tale', lead to some quite remarkable arboreal copulation. So much were these enclosed gardens associated with sensual pleasure that the garden in the French poem *Le Roman de la Rose* becomes a metaphor for the apparently unattainable girl – a metaphor that also recalls the biblical 'Song of Solomon'. Turf benches – sometimes embowered (ravishing word) – and raised walks looked down on flowery meads and gravelled paths, often laid out on a formal plan around a central fountain to maximize the contrast between the artifice of the garden with the untamed forest lurking beyond the boundary. One of the great sensuous pleasures of such gardens, then as now, is the opportunity to enjoy scents which hang undissipated in the still air.

In an age more straitened – in purse, available space and in imagination too – our private place may be smaller, but the elements that combine to make it so desirable are the same. It may be sited where the sun's last rays touch the garden, or where there is a dazzling view. These will draw the owner to his or her den, but then something else is needed to satisfy and soothe, so that the place can work its magic: a secret pool of water, quite still and reflective, perhaps, or a ravishing smell hanging in the air, often exuded by leaves as we gently stroke them* – in itself a vastly therapeutic activity. In this age, the enclosure of our den is unlikely to be cloister walls, rather a trellis or hedge. Even more simply, and an effect that can be achieved in a garden of any size, our secret place might be a tented enclosure created by the boughs of a weeping willow or, on a smaller scale, a weeping silver pear.* We can have our modern bower too – a seat with a trellis-work superstructure over which scented plants ramble, perhaps with some trailing branches hanging over the front and sides to give absolute secrecy.

Moving from such enclosure to the wide open spaces of lawn or pool or terrace will have all the drama of entry upon a stage. Gardens need other, more sociable, sitting places as well. Lovers will need the private place described, only expanded to fit two. We all need somewhere for outdoor celebrations where we can sit and eat in the open air – a civilized pleasure taken for granted in warm climates but prized especially on the rare days in England when it can be enjoyed. There may even be days so hot we need to sit in the shade to be comfortable. Then we can enjoy the Mediterranean delights of sun-dappled table-cloths, glinting wine glasses and the dramatic contrast of sitting in the shade while looking out on to sun-soaked country.

The pleasures of eating in the open are undisputed;* all food and wine tastes better – even leathery barbecued meat and crude wine are made endurable under such conditions. So we may need another space in our garden which will again contrast with the rest – a place for picnics. In Persian, the phrase which most closely approximates to the word 'picnic' is *gol o mol o bolbol*, which literally means 'roses and wine and nightingales'. How nearly can we achieve this idyll? The wine and the roses are easy enough but the nightingales suggest an evening affair, seldom the kind of picnic that suits our climate. But whatever the time of day, picnics need a space not wholly unlike the den described above; it should have bouncy grass filled with wild flowers and herbs; the shade should be broken – which makes fruit trees an ideal canopy, perhaps the roses growing through them, scattering the occasional petal on the sward and the sandwich. It is often assumed that picnics should only be eaten in the countryside, but why not also in the garden?

Like the spaces devoted to eating, those for garden games must be generous. The tennis court needs plenty of room at sides and ends for the athletic player who can cover such immensities of space. A croquet lawn can be any size, shape and condition, provided the Hurlingham rules are suitably adapted. Local hazards add to the interest and call for local rules which, if skilfully devised and only gradually revealed, should guarantee the garden owner victory. Boules can be played on grass, but this tends to soften a game which is at its best when viciously accurate and competitive. Only on gravel and sand can the boule spurt sideways with that sharp click which is so satisfying. On grass the movement is more sluggish and the sound dulled.

The good garden will always tempt the visitor to ask, 'What comes next? And how do we get there?' A wide open space with narrow exits gives the most intense feeling of excitement. If we can half glimpse something through the narrow opening that draws us, then the garden will be doing its own guiding. This may be a fall of water, a beautifully structured and variegated shrub, like *Aralia elata* 'Variegata' or *Cornus controversa* 'Variegata', or dark, enclosed space that contrasts with the wide open area we are leaving. And the transition points between one space and another should be significant. A mere rustic arch will do the job of containing us and framing the next view, but there will be no temptation to linger in it, to appreciate the sense of confinement before we are released into the next area. A double arch, or even a short tunnel, has this effect, particularly if it is covered in a scented climber; nothing causes a garden visitor to dawdle and stop more surely than a sudden wave of scent.

Another kind of variety is the dramatic contrast between light and shade. At Snowshill Manor on the edge of the Cotswold escarpment there is a breathtaking sequence showing the excitement of moving from darkness to light and vice versa. The garden is Anglo-Italian in style, with terraces to make the steep hillside more easily cultivated, so steps and retaining walls in the lovely Cotswold stone quickly establish the theme of the garden. Each terrace is handled slightly differently, but at the northern end, furthest from the house, the terracing gives way to a grass slope cutting down the hillside across all the terraces to end in a ha-ha, as if to remind us of what the site was like before the shaping hand of man touched it. The lowest terrace has a retaining wall to the east, buttressed by a wide raised bed; the rest of the rectangular space is surrounded by walls and farm buildings. There are no shade trees here, so the garden is flooded with light, which in front of the dark, low-roofed barn to the north is sparklingly reflected from a square pool. Blinking from this brilliant light the visitor enters the barn, which is so dark that for a moment nothing is visible. As the eyes grow accustomed to the dark, it becomes apparent that our way leads from the back of the barn through a shaded tunnel of guelder rose (*Viburnum opulus*), underplanted with ferns, hostas, hellebores and bulbs. Here the green light is dappled on the damp ground. At the end of this sombre tunnel a flight of steps leads up into the sunlight again. Nor is this the end of the drama; we find we have not only ascended from shade into light but have escaped from confinement into dizzying space. The steps end on the very edge of the ha-ha, with distant views over the valley to the sheep grazing on the far hillside. This brilliant sequence of light and shade shows the kind of drama that can be achieved in even quite a small garden.

Another variation which has been touched on already is the contrast between confinement and openness, and again, any garden can exploit this by varying the size of the spaces into which it is divided. Hillside gardens can achieve brilliant effects by teasingly allowing visitors a view at one moment and denying them the next. The wonderful garden created by the Vicomte de Noailles near Grasse in the South of France has some witty variations of this sort. The most dramatically satisfying space is the oval lawn immediately outside the house. From here no view was possible over the beautiful hillsides opposite, until the Vicomte's sister, the Princesse de Ligne, had the brilliant idea of cutting down a section of the yew hedge between two giant cypresses. Now the garden combines the repose of enclosure with the drama of the distant views, an effect that is doubly stunning because from the terrace outside the house the twin cypresses and the views are reflected in a circular pool that lies in the centre.

On less dramatic sites and in smaller gardens something similar can be achieved by lengthening the archway between one space and another, and by making it narrow and dark so that the visitor bursts from it into the freedom and light of the next part of the garden.

Entrances and exits inevitably suggest dramatic developments. Gates and doors are sure signs that something interesting lies on the other side. If we go into a new garden and see a door in a wall at the far side, there is an immediate temptation to go at once to open the door – particularly so if a path leads straight to it. Even those who have never read *The Secret Garden* are subject to this temptation. If you want the visitor to linger in the first garden, either conceal the door or make it hard to get to.

Gates and doors can be of many different kinds and each has a different dramatic effect. A solid door, such as the one at the Fortescue garden at Buckland Monachorum in Devon, allows no hint of what lies beyond; it stands in a solid grey stone wall perhaps fifteen feet high and leads from the nursery, with its necessary regimentation, into a paradise of colour and scent. Here are drama and excitement of the highest order. Other gates give tempting hints of what lies beyond: either they are low, to keep animals out or in, or they have slats in place of solid boards. A beautiful example is to be found at Cotswold Farm, a lovely Arts and Crafts movement garden near Cirencester; here, the gate is made of diamond-shaped trellis panels in a solid frame, so that the visitor can only half see the beauties that lie beyond.

Low gates which inhibit the feet but not the eye are useful to define the areas of the garden; these can be whimsical in design, like the lovely wrought-iron gate in the shape of a peacock's tail at Jenkyn Place. Gates, doors and openings often add hugely to the drama of a garden, but can also be misused. The Chinese build moon gates in their walled gardens to frame a view from one part to another; these are circular openings lined with black tiles, which contrast with the surrounding off-white walls. In an English garden such structures can seem inappropriate, particularly if they are not made with the greatest attention to detail or do not focus the eye on an interesting view. In the same way, gates that are too imposing, crowned with urns, obelisks and all manner of finials, can make a small garden lying beyond seem pretentious – our anticipation of something grand has been disappointed, with the result that what we see appears bathetically ludicrous.

Bridges provide another dramatic way of getting from one part of the garden to the next. They can straddle moats, ha-has, a stream, a ditch, a pool or a bog. At their most basic they are just a plank wide and short enough that the user is not terrified to cross. If the bank on the opposite side is higher or lower, it may be necessary to combine a step with a bridge; which can be done by making the bridge in two halves, each of which forms a step up or down. The whole structure is supported by three uprights in the ditch and to these each step is fixed at its appropriate height. The two treads should be absolutely level. A similar structure can be used in simple but longer bridges across water. A plank is laid from the bank and supported by uprights fixed into the bottom of the pool. The next plank can be at an angle to the first so that the transition from bank to island or opposite bank is a kind of zigzag. How much zigzagging is needed will depend on how quickly the owner wants the visitor to cross. The drama of a much-interrupted crossing can be heightened if, at each intersection, a view through the shrubs on the bank is revealed, making the visitor pause.

These simple bridges are no more than a plank supported by an H-shaped structure. More elaborate bridges can have their own drama. Monet's famous rainbow bridge at Giverny, draped in white wisteria, is not only beautiful to look at but beautiful to look from. Only from the bridge do you get the ideal view along the length of the lily pool, with weeping willows providing the swagged stage curtains on each side, to a second, much simpler bridge which acts as the focal point at the far end of the view. In New England there are lovely old covered bridges, whose solid timber roofs give the impression of a tunnel. On such a bridge the traveller may well pause for no aesthetic reason but quite practically – to take refuge from rain or snow. The ultimate development of the roofed bridge is the Palladian bridge, like the one at Stowe. Bridges may also be hinged so that they can rise to let boats through or prevent cattle from straying in. A drawbridge always adds to the drama of a garden and children and the childlike are fascinated by them.

Steps lead us from one space to another and the descent of a particularly grand flight always creates the experience of coming on to a stage. The individual is dwarfed, which is presumably why the great eighteenth-century proprietors loved such broad sweeping steps around their country houses. Most garden makers, though, will be working on a smaller scale. Like tunnels of foliage, steps can be a means of constricting the visitor's movement from one part of the garden to the next, particularly if they are placed between high hedges. There is a moment of great drama as one stops at the top of a flight and surveys from above the next part of the garden to be visited. It is from such a viewpoint that a formally patterned parterre looks so good. Equally exciting is the gradual revelation of a new piece of garden as one rises up a set of steps meet it.

The design of steps can dictate the mood of the garden and of the visitor. Lutyens often used 'in and out' steps, which are designed so that the centre step is a complete circle, while the upper ones are concave, dug into the hillside, and the lower convex, curving out from the slope. Such a design is best used between large, open areas, so visitors are gathered in at the top of the steps, constricted on the middle one, then given space and freedom of choice as they fan out towards the end of the flight. Such steps would seem absurd if the area one was entering was narrow, or if there were no choice of exit at the bottom. At the entrance of his garden at Hestercombe, Lutyens gathers the visitor in from the drive, and at the bottom of his 'in and out' steps there is a choice of paths leading into the garden.

From one formal, small-scale garden to another, less spacious steps may be better. If there is to be a long flight, it is important to remember that they will seem to converge towards the bottom, unless the lower steps are slightly wider than the upper. An excellent example of this control of perspective can be seen at Wayford Manor in a garden designed by that master of Italianate detail, Harold Peto.

Often preferable to a long flight is a set of steps divided by landings where they turn at right angles; in this way, the visitor ascends in slow bursts, with seats on the landings for the elderly and the unfit. If, from the first landing, steps continue at right angles in both directions it is possible to create interesting raised beds, or perhaps a fountain, closely related to the structure of the steps. A design such as this gives a set of steps a presence which is entirely appropriate near the house but elsewhere may seem wrong. In a woodland setting, for example, the steps should be less obtrusive. This will be achieved if they occur at irregular intervals rather than in a flight, and if the risers are made of wood. Half-round timbers treated with preservative make attractive informal risers and can be held in place with wooden stakes driven into the ground.

Formal steps are best built of the same material as the house. Brick is an ideally flexible material in that it can be used for curves or for straight edges (but remember that tight curves will require much cutting of the bricks, a tedious, noisy and messy business). An alternative is to fill the interstices between the bricks as they fan out with terracotta tile. Stone can also be used for curves, although the newly cut edge of stone never looks very attractive. Railway sleepers are excellent for informal steps, though they are messy to cut and handle. If you want your steps to make an impression on the visitor, rather than just fade into the background, be sure that the tread projects about half an inch over the riser; this will create a thin line of shadow under the thread, which gives the whole structure more presence.

A final question to be asked when considering the drama of steps is, should they project from the hill, thrusting themselves out into the space beneath, or should they be more tactfully recessed into the hillside? The answer will depend on what effect you want to achieve and how the steps relate to the surrounding spaces. Recessed steps hold back the view of the next garden until the visitor reaches the bottom, while jutting steps throw the visitor at once into the new space, which can be appreciated straight away from above. If there is no fine view from the top step then the anticipation raised will be disappointed. Recessed steps have the advantage that plants tumbling over the edges can be enjoyed as one descends, and those which divide a border give one the advantage of seeing it from a different angle (along its length) as one begins to descend. By contrast, jutting steps give one the opportunity to see the view and the layout of the next garden from a height, before descending into its midst.

Paths can change the mood of a garden, not only by their breadth or narrowness but by the material they are made of. York paving is noble and formal; gravel flexible and softer to look at. Stepping stones, sunk into the grass so they can be mowed over, are the most tactful way of directing the feet; disappearing round a corner, they are like a paper trail and demand that you follow. Of all paving material brick is perhaps the most interesting. Not only is it available in a variety of textures and colours, but it can be laid in so many different patterns, and each creates a different mood. Laid lengthways along a path, the effect is to hurry the walker to the end.* Laid in a basket-weave pattern, brick suggests a mood of stability and peace in terraces and sitting areas. The herringbone pattern nudges the visitor forward, while suggesting that a dawdling progress might be best. Before laying a brick path it is always best to experiment with different patterns to assess the effects they create.

A path always creates an expectation of something worth getting to. At Painswick House in Gloucestershire there is an extraordinary piece of garden drama, where expectation is wittily disappointed.* From a flat area there is a view through a door in a brick wall, partly veiled by branches; we know there must be a steep descent beyond, but when we go through the door we are confronted by a steep bank and a group of trees which curtain the view of the garden in the valley below. Expectation is whetted and then frustrated because we can't immediately get to the garden, but must zigzag down one of two paths, to right or left, before we reach our goal. Many designers would have seen the steep slope as an opportunity for a flight of steps or a terrace from which to enjoy the whole view. But in this Rococo Garden the obvious is disdained.

So far we have considered the drama of moving through the garden. But there must also be moments of repose or a garden visit will seem no more than a neurotic treasure hunt. The first point of rest will be where the visitor arrives at the house. The garden gate with roses growing over it immediately signals a change of mood from the mundane and the hectic to a calmer, more meditative way of living. If a drive comes to the front of the house, there will be the question of how the cars can be hidden so that they do not spoil the view. (Ideally a car should be able to arrive, deposit a passenger and then move aside, perhaps round to the back door where the shopping has to be unloaded. It is almost always more important to have car access to the back door than to the front.) This arrival space may well be designed rather formally, with evergreen shrubs and solid underplanting that require little attention – though if there are too many evergreens the visitor will feel oppressed. Everyone can remember Victorian rectories with their front doors besieged by giant laurels which seemed to grow on stilts. If the area is dark, shiny leaves will bring in the light, as will variegated foliage and, best of all, water. The visitors will feel a sense of arrival particularly strongly if the entrance area is enclosed. The size of the enclosure must depend on the proportions of the house front; there must be room to stand back and look at the façade – provided it is worth looking at.

Throughout the garden there will be spaces in which the visitor has a similar sense of arrival. The garden has been leading up to this place, so we feel we want to linger here. The mood is achieved when the space is strongly focused on a central feature – fountain, flower bed, sundial, sculpture or aged tree. It is also possible to change the style of the planting so that the visitor moves more slowly; perhaps the colours become stronger or the borders deeper and more intricately planted. But the invitation to linger is most obviously signalled by the provision of a bench.

Seats have many functions in the drama of a garden. They are, of course, for sitting on, and so they must be comfortable – stone seats are not, except in very hot weather; wooden seats must have curved bottoms and backs raked at an angle, or they are not comfortable either. The next requirement is that there should be something to look at from the seat – and perhaps to smell – or there is no reason for the visitor to stop for more than a moment. Often it will have another function, as the focal point of a particular view; then, sitting on the seat, the view can be enjoyed in reverse. At Tintinhull the first, main axis of the garden runs from the house front to a white seat against a yew background, but the seat doesn't immediately catch the eye from the front steps of the house; it slowly reveals itself, half-hidden by the fountain in the white garden.

Designers of the classical period knew all about the drama of gardens and landscapes. Hills and trees concealed, then revealed views; broad vistas alternated with narrow, framed compositions; enclosed spaces were followed by open; and in those days of wealth and grandeur, plant compositions more often focused on a temple or folly than a mere seat.

In eastern Germany there is a splendid example of dramatic landscaping at Wörlitz, one of the first landscaped parks in continental Europe. Temples to Flora, to Venus, a monument to Rousseau, a Gothic house, an Italian farm, a South Sea pavilion (not in the shape of a bubble), all act as the focal points for various compositions, which become apparent as the visitor explores the park. But one piece of dramatic design is easier for us to copy on a smaller scale. The *Schloss* is separated from the lake by a wood which closes the view to the left as the visitor approaches the main façade. How foolish of the designer, we may be tempted to think, to cut off the great view over the water. But as we reach the steps that lead up to the principal entrance, the wood suddenly dissolves, becoming a series of narrow avenues at the end of which the lake glitters. The careful alignment of the trees is only apparent when the visitor looks straight down the lines of them. This brilliant *coup de théâtre* also serves a more practical function, as a barrier against any wind except that which blows straight up the avenues.

All these examples of drama are the result of carefully planned variety; we are surprised by contrasts – between light and shade, and open and enclosed spaces; between spaces to walk through and spaces to sit in; and by the unexpected. All very fine, you may be thinking, in an eighteenth-century park, but what drama can be achieved in a garden a hundred feet long by thirty feet wide?

First, it is possible to make the most of the garden's length by allowing one long view, possibly from corner to corner; this produces more interesting spaces of various shapes than a view down the centre of the garden. At the end of this major axis there may be a focal point – a seat, a sundial, a birdbath, or a door, suggesting access to another garden beyond. This long view will immediately draw the eye, but the feet may have to walk round a pond or a bed in order to reach the garden's end, and in this circumnavigation other parts will become apparent, areas that were previously hidden by wings of hedge or trellis. Each of these subsidiary spaces may have a different character; one will have a fountain, one a fruit tree with spring bulbs in long grass under it, one may be a gravel garden with raised beds for alpines, one a herb garden with thyme or camomile seats. There will be glimpses from one garden to the next, which will draw the visitor on. And the paths will perhaps add to the sense of drama; they may begin by being formally paved, then become less formal gravel, and reach the end of the garden as a close-mown strip through rough meadow grass. They will swell in spaces where the visitor is to pause and contract where the path leads to new excitements through a gap in a hedge. Divisions between one space and the next will be in different materials and of different heights; there may even be holes cut into the hedge to allow a carefully staged preview of what is to come next.

The garden shed will not be hidden but celebrated as the focal point of one part of the garden; we have learned to celebrate the beauty of vegetables but so often the garden shed skulks behind conifers as if it should be ashamed of itself. Such a utilitarian building *could* be fitted out

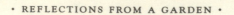

in any kind of fanciful way – with Gothic pinnacles or classical pillars, with trellises and archways; it could even become a romantic bower covered with extravagant climbers. Some people plant the gigantic rose *R. filipes* 'Kiftsgate' over their sheds – one way of emulating the romantic ruins of eighteenth-century landscape gardens, because the rose may well become too heavy for the shed to support. But whatever we do with our sheds, let's not apologize for them. Why should the pedestrian twentieth century not also have its Folly?

CHAPTER SIX

ONLY IN TIME CAN THE MOMENT IN THE
ROSE GARDEN,
THE MOMENT IN THE ARBOUR WHERE THE RAIN BEAT,
THE MOMENT IN THE DRAUGHTY CHURCH AT SMOKEFALL
BE REMEMBERED; INVOLVED WITH PAST AND FUTURE.
ONLY THROUGH TIME TIME IS CONQUERED.

T. S. ELIOT
Burnt Norton

TIME

PERFECT MOMENTS COME IN EVERY GARDEN, though more frequently in some than others. To the very active gardener they may not be of great importance and usually they will be happy accidents, lucky moments when, chancing to glance up, the gardener will see that this or that grouping of plants at the height of their flowering looks exactly right, because of the way the light falls on them.

The moment will be pleasing but fleeting and its transience of little importance when there is satisfying work to be done and the excitement of a tray of newly germinated rare plants to absorb the attention.

This gardener does not plan for perfect moments nor depend upon them for his satisfaction. When they come, often at the end of the day when he is restfully pottering about among the flower beds, he welcomes them but sees them in perspective, for his enjoyment comes all day and every day in his active life as a plant grower.

The more contemplative gardener, seeing the garden as a whole, the design of it, and its nature as a still place of delight and refreshment, will wait and hope for the moment when it seems to achieve perfection. Awareness of when such moments are most likely helps to make them happen; they will not be entirely accidental but anticipated; everything will be planned to encourage them. This gardener will be out in the very early morning and from late afternoon, attentive to small changes in the quality of the light and the atmosphere, as well as to every nuance of the season, which combine to create perfection. Late sunlight will slant for just a few minutes on a variegated shrub placed against a dark, evergreen background; the assertive evening calling of blackbirds and the scream of swifts round and round the rooftops calms and stills as darkness gathers; pale flowers, translucent whites, pinks and chalky blues stand out in the dusk, sharp yellows and oranges are defined separately as dimmer, subtler tones retreat into the spreading shadow. Water on a pool goes dark blue and then black at one particular moment, just as the moon rides up into a clear sky. The dew rises and with it the fainter scents which have been blotted out by the heat of the day. Now, all should be quiet, still; the air is so transmissive that any sharp sound or acrid smell will startle and upset the delicate equilibrium in the garden. Conversation and even company are inappropriate. Such moments are to be enjoyed alone. They are the reasons why some people have gardens.

But if they may be planned and looked for, such moments cannot be preserved. Time will not stand still: we cannot freeze the perfect moment, we may only wait patiently for it to be repeated, and the very intensity of the pleasure such moments give comes precisely because of their transience and their fragility – time is of their very essence. If a garden could be preserved at a moment of perfection and therefore set outside of time, it would become an embalmed garden, lifeless, and pointless as silk flowers.* We do not want to live in unreal places, artificially preserved in a sanitized past (even if we may enjoy a brief holiday in resorts where, we are told, time has stood still).

Gardeners celebrate the influence of time. If we have had a late cold spring followed by a desiccating drought, autumn may be the most soft and golden for years; one poor season will sooner or later be compensated for by another. If plants fall sick and fare ill one year there is always the next, when things may have put themselves right and roses be the best ever. A luxuriant June, when everything seems to flower twice as thickly for twice as long and the whole garden tumbles out in bloom together, can, in the end, sate the appetite, so that even the smell of honeysuckle begins to cloy. On hot, still, over-sweet, leafy evenings then, the gardener may long for the austerity of cold, bare boughs, white rime and the plain penitential garden fare of midwinter. We enjoy what there is, yet long for change, stillness, a rest, like that sympathetic anonymous gardener who cried, 'Hooray! The first frost. The dahlias are all dead.'

There is a continuity about the garden and an order of succession in the garden year which is deeply pleasing, and in one sense there are no breaks or divisions – seed time flows on to flowering time and harvest time; no sooner is one thing dying than another is coming to life. But there are seasons and they come to an end and by late October the growing season is over. Bonfires celebrate and mark a conclusion.* And once, that was that, just as it was for the farmer. After harvest, the land was ploughed and then lay fallow, resting until seed time the following spring. Now, the land is under crop the whole year round – combine harvesters one day give way to the plough next and the seed drill on the day after that. To many people it seems unnatural and they have the same view of things in the garden. They can do nothing to change the intensive nature of modern farming, but they can certainly arrange the garden to suit themselves. They can put it to bed. Everything is cut down, tidied up, vegetables stored, mower and tools cleaned and put away; tender plants are covered or brought into the greenhouse, vulnerable shrubs wrapped snugly in shrouds of sacking or fleece. The leaves are swept up, the very last bonfire darkens at the core and crumbles to ash. A line is drawn under the garden year.

It is a bare place now, muted, green and brown and black, a space of neat shapes and clean lines, to be looked out on from the warmth and shelter of the house. There is a great feeling of resolution and satisfaction at this time, when the year in the garden can be reviewed from the armchair. The next one may be planned and looked forward to but now it is time for a rest and a natural, quiet breathing space. There is also the delight of having the garden indoors for a while, as green branches and berries come in to celebrate Christmas, and the rooms are filled with the sweet smell of forced hyacinths.

But many gardeners do not want an end to things and can never bear to draw a line. For them, articles and books abound on the art and joy of having something growing and flowering in the garden every month of the year. 'Colour all the year round' is the fashion, and the garden is never put to bed for the winter – only parts of it rest while something of interest springs up in another corner.

In large gardens long ago there was a spring garden and a garden for each subsequent season, so that each would be put to bed in turn, and walks would be taken only in the part of the garden that was at its peak; the rest would be ignored – by the owner if not by the gardener. But now, many people want the same patch of earth to perform the whole year round, and this can be achieved by careful planning. The winter aconites can be followed by the early monkshood and these by the lupins and loosestrifes, with the rudbeckias and the lespedeza taking the garden through into the autumn. With a winter-flowering honeysuckle and a holly or two, this same part of the garden can be made interesting all the year round. But is this what you want?

There is no right and wrong about it, no proper way; it is only important for each gardener to discover and decide what is right – whether to draw a firm line under the year and wait for the next, or not. Those who are vague about it, with a foot uneasily in either camp, end up having the worst of both worlds – a mess in the garden, which somehow dribbles on; and a few hastily, yet somehow half-heartedly purchased shrubs planted for winter interest but actually so dull and dingy they fail to earn their keep, and even depress the garden in summer.

Gardens which exist out of time make us uneasy. At the Chelsea Flower Show, gardens exist in defiance of the normal rules: they are created in haste and at great cost for a bare week's display and then disappear for ever, like so many elaborate and labour-intensive castles in the sand. But it is in the nature of those castles to be ephemeral, the whole point of their creation and their charm. The gardens of Chelsea are unreal: they have no past and no future. They may feed our fantasy lives and please the eye fleetingly, but have little influence on the gardens we are patiently making at home. The same air of unreality fills the great tent, breathtaking though the displays are: here we see combinations of plants never produced by any natural season. The spring bulbs have been held back in refrigerators and the summer shrubs brought on in the hothouse, so that they can be placed side by side. The effect is often ravishing but unnerving and slightly surreal because it defies the natural cycle of the seasons. Only in Eden was the influence of time thus suspended – and we have come a long way since then.

Gardeners work with time and sometimes against it, while enjoying the ecstatic moment that seems out of time – the moment which T. S. Eliot, in his recollection of the rose garden at Burnt Norton, called 'the intersection of the timeless with time'. Gardeners work to cyclical rhythms, those of the day and the seasons, and to other rhythms that are directional – the progression of the years and the ageing of the gardener. One of the greatest pleasures of gardening is that we are working to a rhythm so different from that of our non-gardening lives.

In the best gardens there is a sense of order, of spaciousness, of harmony and of tranquillity – a rootedness – and time has many separate rhythms which intersect and correspond and complement one another. Some features are quickly established – stone walls are built and brick paths laid, steps made, urns and statues put in place, trellis erected to form instant divisions, and once established they quickly acquire a permanence and a stability around which the rest of the growing, living, changing garden flows and revolves. But we are required to wait patiently while trees grow, and there is no fast forward button to make the yew hedge double in size overnight. Yet there is always something to occupy us that will provide quicker results: sowing annuals, moving a shrub, or even simply cutting the grass. It takes half an hour to plant a viburnum or an osmanthus, but however sturdy a specimen it may be, it will take years to reach the size at which it can make a real impact on the garden. But spend a whole weekend in October planting a thick ribbon of daffodils to line a long path and you are rewarded by a superb display five months later.

There is something very satisfying about submitting to the disciplines of seasonal tasks, planting the potatoes out on Good Friday, raking up the autumn leaves, or collecting kindling for the winter fire. You are part of a cycle of work that has continued without interruption for generations past. And this sense of the rightness of things is still mildly offended by a book called *Chrysanthemums All the Year Round*, or the sight of raspberries on sale in January (though this is less important to younger generations brought up on international supermarket produce – especially when they are not growers themselves and have no family gardening tradition).

Unseasonal weather disturbs us – frost in May, balmy sunshine in January, for we grew up hearing that summers were always hot and winters white – if only in stories. What we are told of the greenhouse effect upon our future weather is perturbing and not only because we may suffer drought and plagues of giant aphids. We are not certain that we want the compensation of being able to grow olive trees and bananas or plumbago out of doors in North Yorkshire. We feel uneasy – that way, science fiction lies.

Within the cycle of the seasons the cycle of the day turns. In the best gardens the great moment when the shadows fall on the paved walk, or the colours and the structure of the border reach the height of perfection, will be succeeded by other moments which draw the eye in a different direction to other beauties the garden has to offer. Some gardens are even quite different in morning and evening.* The National Trust garden at Coleton Fishacre on the south coast of Devon is made on two sides of a valley that leads south to the sea. In the morning the west side of the garden is lit while the east is in the shadow and the reverse happens in the evening. To see the whole garden at its best you need either to visit for a day or to return at different times. Living with a garden means that you come to understand it intimately, to know its different moods, according to the subtle changes of the season, of the day, and in every sort of weather.

If you live within striking distance of a great garden, regularly open to the public, you come to know every aspect of it by using a season ticket to call in frequently for short periods at odd times, early and late: few gardens are at their best in the middle of the day, when the bright vertical light flattens the contours, drains the plants of their colour and shrinks the shadows that lend drama to the whole composition. For one of the problems of garden visiting is that we only get the snapshot of the moment and miss the deep knowledge of the garden that the inhabitants alone can have. Consider how your own garden changes during the course of a summer's day. You wake very early to drive the rabbits, pigeons and other marauders from the newly planted perennials. The shadows are long and clear cut on the grass, which looks clean and cool with its shimmer of dew. The daisy flowers are shut up tight so that the grass looks newly mown. The low early light penetrates under the trees, catching the grey leaves of a rose which, at other times of the day, has to be sought out; now it parades its beauty at the front of the stage. In this light, you notice neglected corners, where dead ivy leaves have been piled up by a swirling wind. Colours and smells are vivid and fresh.

As the dew dries and the shadows shrink back, the garden retreats into itself; plants hang their heads to conserve energy and moisture. Only the jazziest colours survive the draining power of the sun. A dusty mist dulls the long views.

But then, with the arrival of evening, the garden sighs and comes back to life. The dwindling light changes all the shapes, and the alteration of its angle gives prominence to particular details; plants which release their scent in the evening surround a seat that the gardener has placed to catch the sun as it sets. In the quietness, the pool comes to life with the plop of a frog or a sudden fish breaking the surface of the water. Birds come to drink. Paths and bleached oak gates whiten in the gathering dusk, the boles of the tree trunks hollow mysteriously. So the progress of the day creates many gardens out of one.

While time flows within and around the garden in all its varying rhythms, the apparently timeless moment, perfectly poised, is of deepest importance to the contemplative gardener.* At Knightshayes, in Devon, is a breathtaking garden within the spacious main gardens, which seems immutable in its stillness. It achieves its initial impact by contrast. Just outside, there is a great deal of restless, busy planting in packed beds. Then you go through a yew hedge into a lawned inner garden and feel a slight shock at the stillness and calmness there; your heartbeat seems to slow, your breathing to quieten, instinctively you speak more softly. At the centre is a circular pool with some irises, whose upright, spear-like leaves contrast with the flat pads of water-lilies; at the further side a demure white statue stands in a niche of the hedge. A weeping silver pear hangs over the pool, not at one of the cardinal points in its circle but at the north-west edge. And, apart from two stone benches, that is all. It is the simplicity which makes this garden special, an unexpected simplicity amid such richness. As well as the stillness and sense of timeless perfection. Nothing can be added, moved or taken away without ruining the experience which it offers. It is almost impossible to imagine the leaves ever falling from the silver pear, or the water-lilies dying into brown sludge. 'At the still point of the turning world' time seems suspended.

It is rather the same with some Japanese gardens, in which, with their rocks, water and precisely raked gravel, nothing grows or changes; they are static gardens, for contemplation, and we will only appreciate them if we understand that they have nothing to do with growing or with active gardening and do not require our participation, but exist as places for detached spiritual refreshment. In our gardens water has something of the same function. It soothes, it changes with the seasons, the sky, the light, the time of day and the strength of the wind and yet remains itself, always mysterious.

This sense that part of our garden has escaped the influence of time is important because much of garden making is so obviously ephemeral. 'If only you had come last week' is the gardener's melancholy acknowledgement of time's power. The Japanese garden has permanence. Simple gardens planted only with mature trees and hedges, featuring water or a statue, but otherwise created from grass and paths, are affected only by the outermost, slowest circles of time's movement. Gardens full of plants with flowering seasons or heavily dependent upon annuals in beds and baskets have the shortest life of all, changing within a day, as petals fall, a drought withers and browns. But all gardens in the end are impermanent. Ten years' neglect and what would be left of yours? An ash grove, thickly underplanted with ground elder and bindweed?

Yet we want the garden to look settled, mature, blessed by time as quickly as possible. There is something about an obviously raw new garden that is unattractive. In her poem 'Time', Mary Ursula Bethell spoke for all gardeners:

> 'Established' is a good word, much used in garden books,
> 'The plant, when established . . .'
> Oh, become established, quickly, quickly, garden!
> For I am fugitive, I am very fugitive —

We all know the feeling, but the very word 'established' suggests long, slow, deep-rootedness which even the buying in of thirty-foot-high trees will not achieve. It is certainly possible to plant these at huge expense, and with careful nurturing and much watering they may establish themselves eventually, but while doing so they must be supported by a paraphernalia of guy ropes and stakes and may take several seasons to settle and look as if they belong in their new surroundings.

In the same way we want the birdbaths, urns and statues in the garden to look ancient, or 'distressed', as the antique dealers say. So a few scratches, chips and dents are welcomed, and we cover the raw, freshly cut stone with sour milk, yoghurt and urine to encourage lichen and moss and hide its nakedness as quickly as possible. When looking at the 'distressed' statues in some old garden, the models for the effects we want to achieve in ours, it is hard for us to appreciate that these were once new and might even have been painted in the brightest colours. We want our garden to look established but not to go so far back in taste that we paint our birdbath bright scarlet. Why? Why is it that we want the furnishings of the garden also to look old? Victorians who were newly rich wanted to make themselves look part of the establishment, so they bought their country seats, invented their coats of arms and made the statuary in their gardens look as if it had been there for hundreds of years. And the conservatism of gardeners means that their taste, if not their motivation, has been handed down to us.

But we must not resist all innovation, all change. As the great Gloucestershire gardener, Canon Ellacombe, wrote a hundred years ago,

> I have always noticed that the more a man loves his garden, the more he constantly delights in changing the arrangements, which were, perhaps, good for a time, but which, as time goes on, must give way to others; and the most uninteresting garden is one that has been made to a fixed plan, rigidly adhered to through succeeding years, 'til what may have been good and beautiful at the beginning becomes dull, uninteresting and ugly.

Our gardens will change as we change, as our tastes alter and develop and our experience grows.

Gardens also change as gardeners grow old. Intensively gardened borders have to give way to grass or to less demanding arrangements of shrubs. Raised beds, with firmly built walls, bring the garden up since the gardener now finds it hard to get down. And the garden made by the passionate plant collector in early middle age, when he had to grow every plant that caught his fancy, is now overgrown; all the trees and shrubs he crammed in are falling into each others' arms. Backs stiffen, help is no longer cheaply available; the strength, and even perhaps the will, is lacking to keep all in check.

This ageing gardener lived, like most gardeners, in the near future. Few live for the present but for the better thing that is just around the corner. And the impulse to hope for that better thing is fuelled by remembered experiences of past pleasures. So, as we plant up the garden, we think what it will look like next year or even in ten years' time, but we usually forget what it will look like after fifty years – though the race of great park makers planted for their grandchildren and for subsequent generations, and these men of vision could imagine how their plantings would look a century later; they were unselfish enough not to need instant gratification but also knew that, though their names might be ignored during their lives, a great park is a long-lasting memorial and guarantee of a certain immortality. Parks remain long after gardens have disappeared. We can still enjoy the landscape art of Capability Brown, but of Gertrude Jekyll's work, a century and a half later, almost nothing remains. We have to be satisfied with her own black-and-white photographs, and with the careful restoration of her work at Upton Grey in Hampshire and at Hestercombe in Somerset.

But if gardens are, more than most works of art, subject to time's influence, if that indeed is part of their point, what is to be gained by remaking an earlier garden, using only the plants that were available at the time? Wouldn't Jekyll or Repton have used plants that were introduced later, if they had known them? Can gardens become museums of taste? And how are they to be gardened? Are they to be unlike all other gardens, in that once they are made their development is to be frozen, so that as plants grow old and die they are replaced by exactly the same plant in exactly the same place? The planting plans of the Jekyll garden at Upton Grey are preserved so that the garden we can now visit is as close to her vision as it is possible to get. It is, in fact, closer to what she intended than was the garden as originally made, because Charles Holme, for whom she did the work, ignored some of his designer's suggestions. And what do we learn? That Miss Jekyll had a wonderful eye for proportion and for the potential of a sloping site; that the palette she favoured was not always muted, but that bright colours and tones were used with the greatest care; that she arranged plants to be looked up to against the sky – so *regale* lilies (*longiflorum* in the original scheme) are planted in beds on a plinth up two steps, which invite us to kneel in adoration. Such a restoration is valuable because we can learn from Miss Jekyll's practice rather than the theory expressed in her hortatory and ponderous prose. And in the end it is valuable because the result is an excellent garden.

At Ham House in West London, the National Trust has re-made the garden almost as it was described by John Evelyn in 1678. To the east of the house is a knot garden, enclosed on all four sides by a hornbeam tunnel; to the south is a raised gravel walk, below which are eight rectangles of grass intersected by gravel paths, and beyond this, an extraordinary wilderness, as the term would then have been understood. Six-foot-high hornbeam hedges in a formal pattern create eight walks, which meet at a central circle, but the segments between the walks are treated very informally; here are long grass and wild flowers, with winding mown paths and an occasional, sentry-box-like summer house. This accurate re-creation has been beautifully done and perhaps does give us some understanding of the period of its creation. Nature was by then sufficiently tamed beyond the boundaries of the garden that it no longer seemed a threat; so wildness could be allowed in small doses and carefully contained. The great open space, empty except for the grass squares just outside the house, must have contrasted with the cramped living conditions of the poor. And such spaces were well adapted to fashionable parades. Here the restoration helps us to understand one moment in the development of taste and the history of our civilization.*

And we can appreciate a further stage in this development at Painshill Park in Surrey, where the Painshill Trust is rescuing one of the earliest Picturesque landscapes in the country, complete with grotto, hermitage, and probably the first Turkish tent in a European garden. This last has been re-created in all the extravagant glory of its blue-and-white stripes.

It is not in quite its original position but makes an astonishing eye-catcher at the end of several of the carefully contrived views. The restoration is of interest to the garden historian, but also to those with no interest in the history of taste, because it will broaden their understanding of what can be achieved when one daring man's vision outstrips the fashion of its day. (It should be added that vision without wealth is impotent and that Charles Hamilton ruined himself in creating Painshill Park.)

Is this restoration of historic gardens and landscapes allied to the admiration for past styles of architecture and the attempts to pastiche it in some contemporary buildings? Perhaps nations re-create the gardens of their past, like the buildings, as an exercise in nostalgia, to stimulate a pride in former achievement and to reinforce the glory of the nation, at times when national self-confidence is at a low ebb. In architecture we may be in part reacting against the ugliness of bad, off-the-peg contemporary buildings. But there is something in the nature of gardens which seems to be fundamentally backward-looking. Traditional features recur repeatedly, often until they become the thoughtless clichés of garden design, leading a radical contemporary garden designer to lament, 'I just don't see contemporary art and life reflected in present day gardens. Tradition should be looked at and reinterpreted.' Yet many garden owners want their gardens to be places of escape from the contemporary world, rather than statements of their allegiance to the modern.

In gardens, we long to return to a past world, the imagined idyll of Arcadia and of lost childhood, and this is by no means only sentimental escapism. For many of us have important memories of the gardens of our childhood, which made a profound impression upon our forming imaginations. Our perceptions were heightened then, our sense of mysteriousness and otherness, as well as of beauty, was at its most instinctive and acute. And if there is a particular historical period to which many gardens unconsciously refer, it is surely the summer of 1914, the perfect, golden and seemingly endless summer that marked the end of innocence. That year, Gertrude Jekyll's garden at Upton Grey must have been reaching maturity.

T. S. Eliot understood the curious connection between gardens and memory and how they lead us back to the past without us being aware of it. A memorial garden is a way of taking into the future the memory of someone who is fixed in the eternity of death; the garden grows in beauty and matures, as the lost person would have done. Trees planted in memory of dead children, and the gardens that surround the dead in cemeteries cared for by the War Graves Commission all over the world are particularly poignant. New life arises out of death, time circles on and growth and natural beauty help to console and sustain those who grieve.

In gardens we are reminded of the past and when we walk in them, we choose to reflect upon it and to think of people who have walked there with us; people who gave or told us about particular plants. We remember perfect moments and strive towards a future which will provide us with more of them. We aim to achieve a perfect balance between these twin pulls, so that neither nostalgia nor yearning predominates or is painful. Ultimately, time and the rhythms of the garden satisfy and console.

In the garden time is both enemy and friend; enemy to the gardener in contemplative mood, friend to the gardener in more active mood, enjoying the daily growth of a pan of seedlings. In the perfect garden the balance between these two aspects of time will be satisfyingly maintained. So, as we wander about the garden, looking, noting, comparing, remembering, it becomes clear that, like all gardeners, we are working within a system whose laws are immutable. All we can do is be obedient and co-operative – making small, temporary adjustments.

CHAPTER SEVEN

A SPOT WHEREON THE FOUNDERS
          LIVED AND DIED
SEEMED ONCE MORE DEAR THAN LIFE; ANCESTRAL TREES,
OR GARDENS RICH IN MEMORY GLORIFIED
MARRIAGES, ALLIANCES AND FAMILIES,
AND EVERY BRIDE'S AMBITION SATISFIED.
WHERE FASHION OR MERE FANTASY DECREES
WE SHIFT ABOUT – ALL THAT GREAT GLORY SPENT –
LIKE SOME POOR ARAB TRIBESMAN AND HIS TENT.

W. B. YEATS
Coole Park and Ballylee, 1931

PERSONS

THERE IS THE SEEING OF GARDENS and the making of gardens. Both may have a profound effect upon people.

There are degrees of impact, of course. We may simply be soothed and refreshed by a quiet stroll along the broad paths of one of the great landscape gardens – a Stourhead, a Chatsworth, or a Blenheim, away from the cramped confines of busy streets and our own too-small plot, hemmed in by buildings and noise and other people's fences. But in these parks we can luxuriate in spaciousness, enjoy the wide avenues and gracious groupings of noble trees in their prime: we may have long moments of reflection and contemplation looking across the lake, feel a sense of humility in the face of such grandeur, a sense of pride in our temporary possession of all these acres. If they were not now so generously opened to all comers (and often quite free of charge) such places of wealth and privilege would provoke revolutionary stirrings in the breasts of egalitarians.

Time out at all seasons of the year in parkland landscaped by men like Capability Brown or Repton is time in which to stretch both the limbs and the spirit, and to be made aware of the past and its particular and different priorities and values. At Stowe or Rousham our sense of threat and urgency is smoothed out, nothing hurries us. But very many things may make us stop and stare. We see things in a new and exciting way and so our view of the world is altered. A sudden, perfect combination of site and setting, with planting detail and other features – a wall, an arch or a gate, a statue, a seat or a summer house – seen at exactly the right moment of the day when the light shows them off best can give us the same responsive spurt of pure delight and excitement, the mysterious thump in the solar plexus, as the sight of a great painting perfectly situated in a fine gallery.

Go to Hidcote late on a summer afternoon, when the light has softened but the shadows are razor-edged. There are several breathtaking garden moments to be experienced – and never so great as on one's first visit there, when the shock of surprise and the impact of the sheer nerve of it all are new. (Though, as in any really great garden, familiarity never breeds contempt here; fresh pleasure and delight are always to be had). Walk slowly along the Stilt Garden, across the central grass path or around the gravel paths under the hornbeams: it is enclosed and formal, all the lines are straight and clean. At the end, you are led out of the *allée* into a small gravel area and through a handsome pair of high and quite elaborate wrought-iron gates set between stone pillars in a very high hedge. Within the garden all has been sheltered and green, but as you look up and ahead, not knowing what you are going to find, the light is blue – the deep lavender-grey blue of Housman's 'blue remembered hills' at the end of the day. Go towards it. What garden room will you discover next, in this place, *par excellence*, of garden rooms?

None. You come out from all gardens and there below, lying at your feet and beyond and all around is the open countryside, sheep and parkland in the foreground, the haze of distant Warwickshire and Worcestershire further off. It is not only a surprising moment, it is a curiously exhilarating and releasing one* – you catch your breath and then exhale all at once and release it with delight. Stay and watch the faces of people as they come through the gate and see the view ahead; they almost always smile and lose the rather serious, intense expression of concentration they have worn when walking about the inner gardens.

Just as a great picture can make us see the world through the painter's eyes for some time afterwards, such a garden moment as this can go on affecting the way we see things too. We have been changed by it.

Rarer things may happen. It is not only what we see in a garden that is affecting, it is also what we smell, hear and touch, and sometimes they all combine to create an atmosphere which is quite particular, quite unique. When such moments do come, they evoke various responses; for the religious they provide a spiritual experience – people are moved to awe and humility, to praise and thankfulness, in gardens as in the wider natural world; others have been moved to declare love, to propose marriage, or to make other resolutions and plans which will change the course of their lives.

But there may be nothing so high-flown and dramatic to relate the garden seen to the seer: merely a sense in which colours and shapes and arrangements can alter mood – a fine border in full flush, high, wide and handsome, like those at Crathes in Scotland or The Priory at Kemerton, Packwood House in Warwickshire or Broughton Castle near Banbury, can not only take the breath away, it can also be tremendously cheering and impart a great sense of *joie de vivre*. Whereas too much jazzy, bright planting without respite can irritate and make us want to hurry by; still water almost always calms and soothes, sparkling water enlivens. It's a dull garden that has no effect at all on a person's mood. And when something in a garden has a strong effect upon us, we want to repeat the experience, and not merely by returning to that particular garden again and again: we want to have it, or something as near to it as we can manage, in our own garden, so that it is close to us and available at all times. The shock of surprise and delight, a change from tight enclosure to soft openness, dark to light, formality to wildness, bright busyness to cool stillness – all of these garden effects which so please and delight, satisfy and enliven may be ours, once we recognize them, with careful planning. And so the garden seen becomes the garden made.

Gardens do not exist without people and the garden seen and entered and enjoyed may exert a great influence upon them. But can the garden made in some way express the personality of the maker? Sometimes, perhaps. Certainly, the self-made businessman of Victorian England, and Edwardian gentry with lavish estates, displayed their personalities through their gardens, and it is still possible to learn a good deal about the owner from his pompous, ostentatious garden, all designed for show. Then there is the instant garden of the impatient person, anxious for quick returns; and the garden of the design-conscious, an extension of the owner's stylish house. Such a garden maker is generally as fashion-conscious in plants and gardens as in clothes and cars.

Trying to deduce the character of the owner from the garden is a cheerful and largely harmless pastime for the onlooker. But there may be more to it than that – a second relationship, one between the garden maker and the garden owner – for the two are not always the same. And if a garden expresses more than one personality, the final effect may reflect a degree of compromise or even imperfectly conceal bitter conflict. Few would now wish or can afford to run their gardens in the way of the rich a century ago, when labour was cheap and plentiful. Then, not only great landowners and those with large estates, but the prosperous suburban middle classes too, might have quite large and elaborate gardens which they could enjoy but in which they never had to work. Then, what the owner fancied, he ordered others to achieve; or else he left the entire planning and providing of the garden in the hands of a hierarchy of men, from the head gardener, through the ranks of under gardeners, down to the garden boy. Gardeners are still employed – some private owners can afford to have one or two full time, though most pay for help a few hours a week. Either way, there is still plenty of room for conflict, when garden owner and garden maker battle for supremacy. There is a long and honourable tradition of tension and hostility between the one who gardens and the person who owns the ground. If the garden owner gets his hands dirty, working alongside the gardener for at least part of the time, the battle may merely be a series of sporadic skirmishes over the small practical details – the best way to nurture a particular plant, the right timing of some activity – with occasional brief but bloody flare-ups about matters of design and what looks well next to what. Opinion is anybody's: but the overall plan of the garden will be that of the owner, the vision will be his or hers and the character expressed too.

If the garden maker has long experience, accumulated practical knowledge and wisdom and any pride at all, and especially if he comes from the tough old school of country gardeners; and if the garden owner is full of ideas and designs and sees many garden visions but knows little and does less, the garden scene is set for serious war, generally conducted via long drawn-out rumbling battles and underhand tactics, with the occasional loud explosion. This is hardly surprising; the one who gardens has superior knowledge and skills and, above all, pride, but also feels a day-to-day, year-round intimacy with the plants and their welfare which the owner who does not garden can never wholly share. Both are essential to the garden's existence and each feels possessive of it for different reasons. Money will come into it, of course – it is the owner who pays, and he *is* the owner; his taste will dictate what is grown and where, although the gardener's advice may be taken and a degree of compromise achieved. Often the gardener will know and understand far more about how to make things grow and what jobs should be done when. The garden owner may have a better eye, a clearer overall plan, and has only this garden to think and care about and time to wander round it, early and late, imagining what would look well, noticing the effects of light and shadow, the changes that take place at dawn and dusk. The garden maker will almost certainly have other gardens to work in, not least his own; he only sees this one on Thursdays and has too much to get done, head down, to concern himself with dreams of the future. But he knows a daft idea when he sees one because he also knows the nature of the soil in the different parts of the garden and is experienced with local growing conditions. And he gleefully hugs to himself the knowledge that, *in extremis*, he wields the ultimate power – he can make things die if he really hates them.

But paid, skilled garden help is the exception rather than the rule now. In the majority of modern gardens, owner and gardener are one – or perhaps a couple. How do married garden makers manage? If their relationship began over the compost heap all may be well, but what if something other than gardening brought them together? There was no Mr Jekyll to interfere with Gertrude's carefully organized borders. The only Mrs Johnston in Lawrence Johnston's life was a statue in his garden near Menton; she would never quibble about his daring plantings, or insist on some dreary compromise.

In her more modest way, Margery Fish was a great gardener and plantswoman too, and the books she wrote about the creation of the garden at East Lambrook Manor in Somerset are packed with information and advice. They are written in a delightfully honest, self-deprecatory style and are particularly revealing about the gardening partnership between Mrs Fish and her husband, Walter. His personality is conveyed in the course of her first book, *We Made a Garden*, in somewhat rueful, though usually affectionate terms. (By the time Margery Fish wrote the book, Walter was dead.) Clearly he was a great trial to this gentle, shy genius with plants. Walter emerges as *opinionated* ('When it came to the job of making paths, I discovered that this was a subject on which Walter had very strong views and I had many lectures on how to achieve perfection'); *bossy* ('I should have preferred to fill our cracks with a mixture of sand and fine soil so that tiny green plants would creep along all the stones, but this was one thing Walter would not have at any price. I was allowed a few very small holes in which I planted thymes and Dresden china daisies and the effect was far too neat and tidy'); *a sergeant-major of a gardener*, obsessed with order and tidiness ('Walter would no more have left his grass uncut or the edges untrimmed than he would have neglected to shave'). He was almost certainly unaware of the importance of his wife's quiet contribution to the great English cottage garden tradition ('Walter never showed much enthusiasm for the smaller plants I cherished so lovingly').

But Mrs Fish has a glint in her eye and a vein of steely determination runs as an undercurrent through her prose. She got her way by subtle means in the end, if not during Walter's lifetime, then after his death ('Walter could never be persuaded to have a wisteria because he said they would take far too long to flower. Now, I have two, and both flowered about two years after I planted them').

She knew she was right, and East Lambrook was her garden at last: she is the one it celebrates and commemorates, her obscure little plants triumphed over Walter's vulgar dahlias,* her sweet disorder prevailed at East Lambrook over his regimental straight lines and hard edges.

Perhaps one gardening partner must always be dominant, or how are decisions to be reached about what to plant and where? Can there ever be such perfect harmony in this paradise that agreement is always complete and mutual? In the original Garden of Eden Milton had no doubt who was boss; Adam gave Eve her task for the day – a little gentle staking and tying in; it was just the same at the paradise of East Lambrook: 'When we first started gardening, I was only allowed to watch the great ritual of planting dahlias. I think I was permitted to get barrow loads of manure and cans of water, but Walter would not trust me to do more.' But things changed there. And indeed, now, in the late twentieth-century garden, things are usually the other way round – Eve is boss; Adam is confined to the hard, destructive tasks of mowing and hedging, so suited to his more aggressive fallen temperament. If he is allowed to be creative, the vegetable garden is the limit of his canvas. Sensibly, most couples decide (or at least the situation resolves itself naturally) which partner is to be the authority in horticultural matters – although for some reason gay couples seem to find it easier to plan and work gardens together.

National characteristics may reveal themselves in gardens. The Italians, with their sociable warmth, are less interested in isolated corners where the soul can be cosseted than in theatrical gardens, full of brilliant light and shade, where beautifully proportioned grand stairways tame the hillsides and provide a glorious stage set on which the owner and his train can display themselves; where water is used with masterly control, now thrown up in great jets sparkling against the sombre background of a yew hedge, now purling down a cascade or, as at the Villa Lante, taught to run in a channel down the centre of a marble dining table, where it acts as a wine cooler. Water was used to play tricks on unwary guests, to cool the air, to power musical instruments; anyone who could afford to use a scarce resource like water in such non-utilitarian ways was clearly a god among men.

There is less braggadocio about French gardens. They celebrate the dominance of man over nature with their great avenues and straight lines, though the emphasis here is on clarity rather than display. And the typical French public garden, with its box-edged gravel walks under tightly pruned limes, seems invented for perambulating rational debate, rather than swaggering ostentation.

A Chinese courtyard garden isolates the owner from the world but then imports a landscape that is miniaturized and idealized; piles of rock or massive monoliths reflected in a still pool remind the visitor of the mountain retreats of hermits and sages. There is constant drama in even the smallest garden, like the Wang Shi Yuan in Suchow; a confined space is followed by a generous courtyard; through openings in the internal walls, glimpses of what is to come next tempt and tantalize; often a choice of path is offered – one will lead up a rock pile from which there will be a new view down over the whole garden, while another will continue straight along the side of a pool – this is almost the choice between a town and a country walk. There are few plants, but these gardens seem to focus on the celebration of pleasure – wine and good company certainly. A simple delight in such elementary sensations as listening to the wind in the pines, combined with the most sophisticated understanding of space and garden detail, seem typical of this ancient civilization.

And what do English gardens show of the national character? As you might expect of a nation addicted to compromise, the gardens are rarely bold or imposing. Softness of colour and blurring of outline are more typical. Perhaps this is because, in our damp island, the light is seldom sharp enough to illuminate the brightest tones, or to cast those knife-edged shadows that add to the drama of Italian gardens. Miss Jekyll's celebrated planting in drifts – irregular groups of plants – is another kind of compromise: it avoids equally the rigid artifice of the broderie parterre, and the natural, dotted effect of an alpine meadow. The word 'soften' is one of the commonest in the basic garden design primers; nothing stiff or regular is allowed, as if the garden's form must always be concealed: hard path edges are to be 'softened' by plants pouring over them; walls are not celebrated for their intrinsic beauty, but instead are 'clothed' in climbers. The Chinese, by contrast, hardly ever plant climbers against walls; in their gardens these are screens on to which shadows are cast in winter, and throughout the year they act as neutral backgrounds, highlighting the form of a tree or shrub planted in front. Our 'soft' gardens are often reminiscent, even sentimental. They look back to an age of stability, back to a Never-Never-Land of cottage gardens (did they ever look like those in Helen Allingham's paintings?); to an age when gardeners were cheap, so the perfection of the edging and the absence of weeds is not to be wondered at. Then the English were effortlessly superior, with an Empire that spanned the globe and provided an unrivalled range of plants. Is it significant that, as Britain's political influence diminishes, we spend more and more public money on restoring historic gardens instead of making new ones?

Of course, any given garden may be an amalgam of tastes and fashions and reveal nothing other than the type of stock in the nearest garden centre, the garden style of the previous owners, overlaid one upon the other, or the fads of a fashionable garden designer filtered down through articles in magazines. But sometimes one personality, that of the garden owner and maker, is obvious and expressed in the garden for every visitor to see. Walter and Margery Fish typify the two opposite extremes. In some gardens, of which Walter would so have approved, every edge is trim and the earth between is hoed and raked – almost curry-combed, lest a weed appear. But another sort of gardener allows plants to flop over all the edges, over themselves and into other plants; foliage has to be moved aside to show you a particular treasure which is so far from being on parade, that it is invisible until proudly brought forward. It is the hoe that divides such garden makers; hoers love this tool because it cleans the ground of intruders, giving more space and light to the chosen flowers that are to be displayed against a svelte brown background. Floppy gardeners hate hoes because they say it robs them of the serendipitous arrival of something they had not planned for. They like hand weeding, because only thus can they distinguish between the seedling weed and the seedling treasure. By refusing to hoe they are in no danger of beheading a rarity, and if the hand weeding is never complete, they don't really care.

But where is the line to be drawn between sweet disorder and chaos? The answer is partly a matter of belief and even of conscience, and partly one of temperament. Many gardeners are threatened by disorder; they feel that their artistry will be concealed if the garden is not well spaced, well staked and weed free. Others like the illusion that their gardens are beautiful by chance, that nature has done more than they have; they allow some self-seeders to grow – campion, for example, because the pink flowers harmonize well with the colour theme in that part of the border – but do not give an intrusive sow thistle the same accommodating welcome. The floppy gardener's great defence of self-seeding plants is that the borders are stuffed so full that no earth shows and so weeds do not find any easy tilth to grow in – or if they *do*, often a herbaceous plant will flop over to hide their shameful intrusion. (Bindweed is an exception; it will advertise its presence by climbing the tallest delphinium and spreading its brilliant white flowers to flash a signal of triumph in a visitor's eye).

How much do gardens tell us then about human character? Are all cowed gardens, where the plants are bullied into order, the work of anal retentives? Are straight edges the sign of a tense personality? Do floppy gardens give evidence that their creator is in search of that ideal but ever-receding childhood paradise, before manners and etiquette stifled all spontaneity? Or do gardens merely tell us about the taste and perhaps the financial circumstances of the owners after all?

Money is a great revealer of character, in gardens as in other areas of life. Some people do not have any but don't let that stop them from creating most beautiful gardens, rich in variety of plants. They manage it with careful taste, good planning, green fingers, years of experience, knowledge acquired from listening to and watching others, and unremitting hard work. Such gardeners see no need to spend much; they save seed, take cuttings, make compost, swap plants with others, look after their tools meticulously, re-use string and mend their own fences. If they won the pools, it would make no difference to the way they gardened.

Others use their money judiciously, to save themselves time or to buy a little of the best advice, and enjoy a good spending spree at a plant sale every year.

And then there are the sort of people who lavish a lot of money on their gardens because they are show-offs. If some practical garden knowledge and common sense do not season the fat of their bank balances, they are at the mercy of every landscape firm, garden designer or supplier of artefacts and expensive plants, and indulge in every latest fad and fancy – the costlier the better – buying the wrong thing for their particular soils or situations, and feeling angry and hard done by when it fails to thrive. There is always fun to be had from watching a fool and his money being parted. The very rich man can have exactly what he wants and where he wants it. He may have a Japanese garden in the middle of the Cotswolds; excluding the rolling hills behind high walls, he can create an elaborate escape into a world of mossed mounds, raked gravel, stone lamps, bamboo, pools and streams. The administrator, returned from India, may wish to be reminded of the land he has left, so he creates, at Sezincote in Gloucestershire, a fantasy Mogul palace and a garden with canals and raised fountains and basins. The collector of Italian sculpture may want his garden to remind him of that country and to be an open-air museum to house his collection. So Harold Peto at Iford adapted the terraces of his hillside to make an Anglo-Tuscan garden. Given adequate funds and ambition you can even, like James Bateman at Biddulph Grange, have the whole world in your garden.

But the expression of personality in a garden need have nothing at all to do with money or, for that matter, with acreage. Inventiveness and ingenuity, the love of plants and an affinity with them, coupled with a refusal to be restricted by received gardening tradition and conventional wisdom, daring, boldness, a lack of concern for the restraints of the rule book – eccentricity even – are all revealed in the great, tiny garden created in North Oxford by Mrs Anne Dexter. In a space of twenty-seven yards by seven she has created a canyon garden of astonishing beauty. The central path winds gently and has been dug out to create a greater sense of height in the beds at either side, into which the top soil has been gathered. This is the garden of an indomitable plantswoman – she is not to be denied her favourites, somehow room must be found for them. Carefully chosen trees have to be pruned, severely, to keep them to an appropriate size. Every inch of space is used and, because the horizontal dimensions are constricted, Mrs Dexter has made a vertical garden. Clematis climbs through everything. The deep blue C. *eriostemon*, and the velvet purple C. 'Royal Velours' nod down at the visitor from above. Even the tiniest plant is carefully placed and admired because the raised beds bring it close to the eye. This brilliant garden is a triumph because the restrictions of the site have been turned into advantages by the imagination and determination of the owner.

Ingenuity of character and determination not to be thwarted by circumstances are often revealed in the gardens which are idiosyncratic because their owners require them to do particular things. A Hertfordshire garden has chalk banks, imported by the lorry load, so that the right wild flowers will grow to provide food for the butterflies that are the owner's chief delight. In the Cotswolds, another owner has adapted his garden to the physical difficulties that accompany his increasing age. He has problems with his knees, but he has not allowed this to stop him gardening; he merely does it standing up and, to do so, has created a garden on the top of a retaining wall, which is tended from the lawn five feet below. Gardens can be made for the especial enjoyment of other people with particular needs – scented gardens for the blind, and gardens of raised beds which are easily tended from wheelchairs.

And gardens and gardening may transform the lives of people in another special circumstance – those who are on their own, probably not from choice but because they have been widowed or otherwise bereaved. Many the man or woman who has been left with a garden that was once looked after exclusively by a partner, now gone, and who at first sees to its needs only minimally and very much out of a sense of duty, knowing how the other person would have been saddened to see unweeded and overgrown flower beds, unpruned shrubs, an unmown lawn. But soon comes the realization that gardening is, at the very least, something to do with time that may now hang heavy; and that jobs outside are a pleasant way of filling the empty hours at the end of the day when companionship is most missed. So gradually, what begins as a chore may become a pleasure; interest may grow and new dimensions be added. The absent gardener never bothered with a greenhouse, perhaps, or got to grips with hardy perennials, but preferred everything annual and bedded out: the one who is left alone may discover, say, a delight in alpines and join a club to learn more about them and share the enthusiasm. Growing alpines leads to the society of other alpinists, spring holidays may be taken to Switzerland, where they are seen in the wild and at their most breathtaking. A whole world opens up, not just of gardens and gardening, but of new friends too.

Gardens satisfy both the need to be happily and constructively alone and the wish to have company and a shared interest – there is no corner of the country which is far from a garden club, or branch of some specialist garden society. Many places are close to horticultural colleges, which offer day and evening, full- and part-time courses for gardeners at every stage. Garden tours with like-minded companions are advertised in gardening magazines. There are few activities which fill time so satisfyingly and fulfil a person's needs.

Nostalgia may be the reason why so many people come to gardening in middle age. The departure of children, and so easier financial circumstances, together with the desire to unwind from the stresses of mature responsibilities, may also be factors. We wish, too late, that we had planted more trees while we were young, but such regrets are balanced by the satisfactions of working within the rhythms of nature to an end beyond ourselves, while being aware that what we create is the most fragile kind of art that man has devised. As we move into old age the demands of the garden gradually become too many and too great; it begins to slip from our control. You can see this sometimes, visiting the garden of someone elderly; it has come to maturity with them and then grown old with them; paths are invaded by sweeping branches of trees; self-seeders take over, as their invasions begin to go unnoticed; shrubs grow into each other, creating impenetrable thickets. The garden needs more than a bit of clearing; by now it needs regeneration. But that will be a task for younger hands and for an owner who does not dote so fondly on so many treasures, given over the years by old friends, long gone, or collected on visits to many corners of the world.

Meanwhile, the beginning gardener soon discovers the generosity of the world he has joined and so becomes aware that the practice of gardening seems not only to reflect but to influence personality, for nothing seems too much trouble to the gardener. 'Of course you can come and see the garden. I love taking people round.' No mention of the fact that the weary owner is leaving for America at six the same evening, or that you are the tenth person this week to make the same request. You are just welcomed warmly and shown round, all the time learning from someone who has years of experience of the most useful kind. And such people are usually as generous with their plants as with their time. 'You like that? Do have some cuttings.' And so, interesting plants are distributed and your garden fills with them and simultaneously with memories of generous givers. It is impossible to forget someone whose plant is flourishing in your garden.

Perhaps gardening does make us more generous: and it surely encourages us to be humble. In our mind we have such visions of perfection – colour schemes of the greatest subtlety and precision, shrubs arching delicately over rustic bridges, streams forever flowing in the background. But nature has other ideas: plants that flourish in a neighbour's garden stubbornly refuse to establish themselves in ours. A rabbit eats the seedlings of some rare salvias. A phlox that all the books say grows to four feet does not stop, this wet summer, until it has reached six – obliterating the view of the shrub tastefully arranged behind it. Showers leave the roses looking like washing-up mops; frosts bite and blacken the blossom; squirrels gnaw the bark of specimen trees. Why do we go on bothering and trying, when at times it all seems so hopeless? Our proudest plans are wrecked. But humbly, hope triumphing over experience, we begin again, and with any luck a bit wiser than before. Perhaps there is a connection between humus and humility as close as that between the ground and the weeder's knee. True gardeners, as opposed to exterior decorators,* always seem modest, as if they realize there is a magic about growing things over which they ultimately have no control. Reginald Farrer, the great alpinist, wrote, 'The true gardener is the reverent servant of nature, not her truculent, wife-beating master. I think the true gardener, the older he grows, should more and more develop a humble, grateful, and uncertain spirit, cocksure of nothing except the universality of beauty.'

But if making a garden is often exasperating and frustrating, there can be no doubt about the therapeutic value of growing things. Retiring to the greenhouse, allotment or potting shed is a way of claiming some private time. And what is done there is so peaceful – unless the neighbour is rotovating his patch or using a power saw. The silence is itself therapeutic, particularly by contrast with the way most of us spend our lives. After the fret of the crowded railway carriage, bus or tube, after the frustrations of the endless traffic queues; after the jostling, the dirt, the ill temper, here is a place of soothing, unhurried, tranquil activity. There is no stress in sowing seed in a beautifully prepared tilth, or in taking cuttings, very neatly and precisely, with the sharpest of knives. Our cuttings may take, our seeds come up, everything may thrive – or not. But it does not help to worry about it. And the activity itself is pleasing and quite harmless and, at best, we shall have a lot of beautiful, sturdy plants to be proud of – far too many, so that we can give some away to friends.

Plants are your progeny and, just like a family of human children, make demands that you may sometimes resent. Looking after both teaches you to put something else before yourself. And then there are the virtues of gentleness and patience to be cultivated along with the young plants. Seedlings require very careful and unhurried handling when being potted on. Some gardeners need absolute quiet at this stage, which always encourages a reflective and even philosophic mood; others find a little background music helpful. Either way, the mind is quieted, the attention is engaged just sufficiently by the business in hand, and a deeper level of consciousness can work freely. The repetitive moving of seedlings from seed tray to pot; the trimming of cuttings before they are dibbled into the earth; the sowing of seed at just the right intervals, are all tasks conducive to such thinking. It is surprising how often some problem – of design, of conduct, of judgement – unknots itself during such tranquil gardening periods.

Are gardeners ever proud? Are they allowed to be? Why ever not? Pride in a garden may be exactly like pride in one's children; both can be shown to others with great pleasure and delight and also a deep sense of privilege. 'Show' is not the same as 'show off'; pride in the garden when it has been brought up to its best need not be boastful, and the gardener, as much as the parent, will have more sense than to claim 'alone I did it'.

Perhaps the best attitudes and the best kind of garden pride are conveyed in the character of one particular gardener, lovingly described by Mr Allwood, the great carnation grower, in his book *The Nobodies*.

Many years ago, after I had given a lecture at the People's Palace, Whitechapel, a rather shy, faltering individual came up to me and said, 'Would you like to see my garden?' I thought to myself, 'What kind of garden can he have right in the heart of the largest city in the world, how could anyone make anything which could be called a garden among all these great buildings?'

Presently he was leading me up and up flights and flights of stairs and through dark passageways to the top of a tenement building. There I saw a wonderful garden. The whole flat roof of the building was a garden full of blooms and vegetables. Flowers of every kind seemed to be everywhere: plants growing on little shelves all over the place, cunningly constructed: many pots containing all sorts of plants, such as heliotropes, fuchsias,

carnations, geraniums and pinks, growing round the edges of
boxes, with the flowers hanging down and filling the air with as
rare a fragrance as ever one enjoyed in the country. All I could
say was, 'How wonderful!' But he said apologetically, 'It is
nothing. The air is not too good and the sun does not always shine
so that some plants are rather weak. It is not like the country.'

But there was evidence here of much loving care, infinite pains
and much patience. I watched how his hands touched his plants,
how he fondled them with the sympathy of the enthusiast. He
could not hide the touch of pride in his eyes. He told me with joy
the history of every plant and its peculiarities, the obstinacy of this
one, the thirst of that one and the trickiness of yet another. There
was not a square foot of space wasted. There was even a
vegetable marrow which he showed me with great pride, growing,
in a box of earth close to the chimney wall and trained up trellis
work. As he said, 'there is plenty of room in the sky'.

CHAPTER EIGHT

THE JUNE NIGHTS ARE LONG AND WARM; THE ROSES FLOWERING; AND THE GARDENS FULL OF LUST AND BEES, MINGLING IN THE ASPARAGUS BEDS.

VIRGINIA WOOLF

Diaries

SENSES

THERE ARE MANY DEEPLY CIVILIZED PLEASURES to be found in Chinese gardens, but perhaps the most remarkably un-Western is the pavilion whose name focuses the attention on a particular sensuous pleasure – so, in the Yu Yuan in Shanghai, there is a Pavilion for Viewing the Frolicking Fish; the terrace of the pavilion hangs over the water and a seat with a railing at just chin height makes it easy to imagine hours passing in a delighted trance, observing the fish frolicking in the pool below. In the Garden of the Incompetent Official at Suchow the visitor finds other senses catered for: a pavilion is dedicated to hearing the Wind in the Pines and another to the Fragrance that Comes from Afar – the fragrance of lotus blossoms. What subtle understanding of civilized living and what careful analysis of the diverse pleasures gardens have to give!

Some Western garden makers are reluctant to analyse the kinds of sensuous delight their gardens can offer – perhaps a romantic fear that dissection of pleasure will result in its destruction holds them back. Or perhaps this is an age of such overwhelming visual stimulation that we undervalue the pleasures offered by our other senses. It is certainly true that sense impressions from the garden usually come intricately interwoven so that it is hard to separate them; the smell of the earth after the first warm rain of summer blends with the sight of apple blossom and the sound of mating birds bursting themselves in song. But some pleasures are so distinctive, it is hard to understand why they are not noticed. The silky leaves of the tibouchina are a delight to touch throughout the year, but the catalogues mention only the astonishing beauty of its deep indigo flowers. Perhaps we need a list that stresses the tactile pleasures that plants offer; think what might be in it – the widow iris with its sleek black falls, *Dorycnium hirsutum* (its second name suggests unshaven chins, but its leaves are as smooth as silk), the rigid, sculpted foliage of *Viburnum davidii*, the leathery *Clematis armandii* and so on. The reflective gardener will not undervalue the pleasures of any sense, and will plan for these pleasures at all seasons of the year.

'Midwinter spring is its own season', according to T. S. Eliot, 'Sempiternal, though sodden towards sundown.' For many gardeners winter is a season that seems all too damply eternal, but there are sensuous satisfactions to be had even at this low point of the year.

The University Botanical Garden at Cambridge demonstrates superbly how beautiful and colourful a winter garden can be. Dogwood stems shine in the damp, dim light, the bright red of *Cornus alba* 'Westonbirt' and, more subtle, the olive green of *C. stolonifera* 'Flaviramea', and the trunks of birch – silver (*Betula utilis* or *jacquemontii*) or cinnamon (*B. albosinensis* var. *septentrionalis*). Frost etches patterns on evergreen leaves; every vein on the beautifully marked leaves of *Viburnum davidii* stands out. And trees with contorted forms, perhaps the corkscrew willow (*Salix matsudana* 'Tortuosa'), or 'Harry Lauder's walking stick' – the contorted nut – look their best in winter, waving their twisted arms against a grey-washed background of wind-driven clouds. Then there are flowers – in deepest winter the golden, spidery bunches of the witch hazel (*Hamamelis mollis*), which must be planted with a dark background to show up well, or the unfurling falls of the winter iris (*I. unguicularis*).

The beauty of many gardens, like that of many people, derives from their bone structure. Summer, with its overflowing bounty, blurs the clean lines; in winter the skeletons reappear with all their austere beauty. The pattern of a brick path, the well-proportioned steps, the

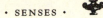

satisfying form of a gate – all these come into their own when the frothy lushness of summer has passed, and the forms of bare trees, their branches and twigs spread out like a complex system of veins and arteries, have a particularly mysterious and deeply satisfying beauty. Gardens formally patterned with evergreens, perhaps cut into topiary shapes, look their best in winter, particularly on bright frosty mornings, and there is more time to appreciate the unexpected blossoms which surprise us with their colour. Winter pleasures come singly and unexpectedly; perhaps then our gardens most nearly resemble Chinese gardens, with their sparing use of plants and emphasis on proportion.

Thoughts of hamamelis* lead us on to the smells of winter, a season well endowed with scent if shrubs are carefully chosen. The darkest days of late December and January can be perfumed with Christmas box and wintersweet (*Sarcococca* and *Chimonanthus*) – the smallest sprig of either will fill a room with scent for a week or longer; as will the winter-flowering honeysuckles: *Lonicera fragrantissima* earns its superlative for smell, but the later-flowering *L. setifera* has both scent and beautiful flowers. If you have a damp piece of ground, perhaps in the shade of a fence beside a path, you can grow the winter heliotrope (*Petasites fragrans*). This will provide the scent of vanilla in late winter, and its fine glaucous leaves will give you pleasure in the summer. But beware – this plant is an imperialist and will colonize any territory to which it has access; some call it a thug – but how many thugs do you know that will delight your nose at thirty-five yards?

In the garden it is harder to satisfy the sense of touch and taste in winter. But you can revel in the slippery, even slimy feel of dead herbaceous matter (this clinically comprehensive noun is so appropriate to the fetid, indefinable mass you have to cope with when clearing the borders). And some foliage is delightful to touch if you dare expose your hand to the sneaping winds: for example, the crinkly leaves of *Cistus corbariensis* or the leathery ones of garrya; and honesty seed pods are smooth as ice. By contrast the foliage of *Lonicera giraldii*, an evergreen, is as soft as rabbit's fur. Tastes of winter include apples wrapped in newspaper, wrinkled and aromatic, and bletted medlars. Garden sounds to treasure are the rare fragments of birdsong – indignant sparrows, sociable robins and crazed blackbirds – or the rattle of bamboo stems against each other as they are whipped by the gales, and the whispering of the few leaves clinging to the beech tree. In the bitterest weather the crunch of footsteps in frosty grass and the creak of compacting snow under the boot are too rare sounds in our increasingly mild climate; they are among the cleanest and sharpest of winter delights.

But meanwhile, the garden is still providing pleasures for the house – branches of viburnum and winter cherry (*Prunus subhirtella* 'Autumnalis') opening in the warmth and scenting the rooms, pots of white cyclamen along the windowsill competing with the snow beyond the glass. Christmas brings its own particular sensuous pleasures – the pungent, resinous smell of the evergreens that decorate the house, the heavy scent of forced hyacinths and the sharp prick of holly as you try to arrange its awkward angles behind a picture.

And there is an oral pleasure for the privacy of the winter fireside – trying out the new names of exciting plants which the catalogues are promoting; if you are planning to add to your trees, now is the time to practise saying *Metaseqoia glyptostroboïdes* so that next summer it rolls off your tongue with satisfying and astounding ease. Other names for familiar plants can also give pleasure: honesty in Latin is *Lunaria annua* – the moon plant, because its seed heads look so like the full moon; the cool, pebbly roundness of the botanical name conjures up more of the plant's character than the common one. Now is the time to have a go at saying *Paeonia mlokosewitschii*, which cowards have nicknamed 'Molly the Witch', and to get your teeth into crunchy zauschneria.

Spring arrives with the green-ruffed, golden winter aconites (*Eranthis hyemalis*), which thrust themselves up through mud and snow, yet are always gleaming with health when they open. Equally heroic, and undaunted by any freak of the weather, are the Lent lilies, *Helleborus orientalis*. Their delicate freckling and colours, ranging from plum to clearest white and on to buttercup yellow, give them an entirely false air of purity – in fact they interbreed indiscriminately.

Pools of blue will soon catch the eye – scillas, such tiny bulbs that they are easily dug up and moved. And there will be daffodils, of course, 'that take the winds of March with beauty'. Then, as the trees begin to come to life, the grey, unfolding goblet-like leaves of the whitebeam, *Sorbus aria* 'Lutescens', and the quince (*Cydonia oblonga*) gleam through the clear, spring air. The bare, black branches in the hedges are first covered with a gauzy softness – is it green or yellow or even, with poplars, brown? – before the leaves take on distinct shapes and colours.

The variety of smells is sustained and developed with greater and greater intensity as the earth warms up, and the soft spring rains fall. *Clematis armandii* with its gleaming white flowers smells deliciously fresh, while mahonia has a heavier, almost sickly fragrance which wafts in clouds far over the garden. *Osmanthus delavayi*, that super-elegant shrub with small, bottle-green leaves, smells less overwhelming, slightly lemony and astringent. But with the hyacinths the scents begin to reach a climax; their perfume is unmistakable in its richness. One smell above all others signals the advent of summer – that of the balsam poplar (*Populus balsamifera*). If you have one anywhere near the house, on a warm, still day in late spring you will be embalmed in a honey scent as you open your door – one that is so all-enveloping you can scarcely detect its source.

The spring smells excite the animals also, and the more your garden attracts wildlife, the greater the variety of sound will be. Birds call for mates and chatter angrily at rivals, rustling busily in the evergreens and ivy; frogs plop into the pond and serenade each other throatily on warming evenings; thrushes thrash the life out of snails, their hammerings carrying over the still garden. This is a busy time for gardeners, but there should be a moment to stroke the glossy leaves of the spring leucojums, and the black falls of the hermodactylus, which look and feel so like the fur of a black cat.

And taste? Has anyone ever felt surfeited on asparagus? Most of us never have quite enough. There is no taste more luxurious, and the act of eating it is so satisfying, with butter dripping from your chin and running up your arms to the elbows.

Summer is the season when we are most able to enjoy all the sensuous pleasures of the garden. Food tastes better for being eaten in the open air, so the horticultural sensualist will have a place for outdoor eating. But since we must be comfortable when at table, the place must be protected from chill winds, intrusive smells and flies. The garden itself provides a multiplicity of scents at this season: grass mowings with their narcotic heaviness, the gloriously pervasive sweetness of philadelphus (which used to be called 'mock orange' – the smell is so like that of the fruit tree it is easy to see why), and the unexpected chocolate smell of *Cosmos atrosanguineus*. Then there are the old-fashioned roses with their range of scents, from the delicate sweetness of 'Fantin-Latour' to the lemony *rugosa* 'Blanche Double de Coubert'. And for the dedicated sensualist, what greater reminiscent pleasure could there be than reclining on a thyme or camomile seat?

As the slow dusk falls, the rising dew evokes quite different smells. A relaxed tour of the garden in the waning light with a watering can releases all kinds of wonderfully aromatic scents. Against the wall the night-scented stocks send out perfumed blandishments to the insects that pollinate them. Smellers like these are best planted near a door or under a window. Honeysuckles too will climb to peer in at your bedroom and perfume it as you go to sleep. The burning bush (dictamnus) is even more astonishing: it releases clouds of scent into the warm night air, and these can even be set ablaze, as its name suggests. A wall, or even better a walled garden, seems to preserve all the day's scents in a glorious mixture, a real anthology of what you may have ignored during the hours of daylight.

The pleasures of sight in the summer garden are too numerous to list; many come from colour and its subtle blending, but some are simpler and easier to create. One of the few good reasons for keeping an immaculately barbered lawn is to provide a smooth screen for the shifting pattern of leaf shadows. And an avenue or, less ambitiously, a line of trees, can provide enormous satisfaction late on a summer evening when the shadows are thrown in perfect parallels across a paved walk.

The sounds of summer can also be planned for. A lime tree in your garden will not only provide you with heavy scent but will be abuzz with every kind of bee during its flowering season; some limes – the weeping silver lime (*Tilia* 'Petiolaris'), for example – drug bees with the powerful scent of their flowers. There will be birdsong in your garden from morning to dusk and later, particularly if you have planted some evergreens for the birds to shelter in during the winter. Dragonflies delight the eye with their flashing, electric-blue wings, but they are often first detected as they rattle their way through the stems of bamboo growing near your pond. Plants also contribute to the range of sounds: on a very hot afternoon you will hear mysterious poppings from your borders, like a particularly efficient cap pistol, but this is not some delinquent infant at play, it is the seed heads of *Euphorbia characias wulfenii* bursting.

The tastes of summer are numberless – strawberries, raspberries, blackcurrants gleam with health; the fruit bends down the stem so that grabbing a handful is charitably relieving the bush of its burden. Herbs and juvenile vegetables offer the same irresistible temptation to reach out and eat them on the spot in all their crunchy freshness. The nutty taste of salad vegetables is one of the defining sensuous pleasures of summer. There is one less familiar ingredient of salad that is as delightful to the eye as to the palate – the buckler sorrel (*Rumex scutatus*), so called because its leaves are shield-shaped. This is a low grower which spreads sideways. The leaves are glaucous and marked with a silver pattern disturbingly like a snail's trail. Despite this, they look decorative in a salad, and have an unexpected tang of lemony acid. Broad beans should be eaten young, scarcely shown the hot water and served with butter and black pepper. There is hardly a flavour to equal it.

In summer much tactile pleasure is derived from lifting flower heads to smell the perfume, and in satisfying one sense the committed sensuous gardener will not ignore the other delights on offer; enjoy the velvet texture of the deep-red rose 'Étoile de Hollande' as you hold up its head to sniff it, and stroke the silky flanks of the *regale* lily as you bend your nose to it. Tactile pleasures can be derived from foliage too. The leaves of *Lobelia tupa* are a soft matt green and delightfully rasping to the touch, like a piece of old linen. Quite different to the smooth almost rubbery foliage of *Coronilla valentina glauca*, a shrub often overlooked among the winter flowerers – perhaps because it flowers for such a long time.

Autumn is most obviously the season of tastes and smells. Quinces spread their exotic, oriental perfume through any room in which they are left. Hands are stained like Bluebeard's with the juice of blackberries. There is a great poignancy about many of the latest flowers of the year. Some are designed to withstand the gales – the Japanese anemone, for example – but some seem too limp, like many of the asters. Most delicate and astonishing of all is the tiny-flowered *Saxifraga fortunei*, which holds its starry flowers up to the winds as if in defiance. And it flowers far into October.

The purple blossom of *Lespedeza thunbergii*, cascading down a bank, is one of the great sights of autumn, and then, with the first frosts, comes the tree display. The leaves of *Parrotia persica* give us a firework show, so many colours it is impossible to describe. The golden maple, *Acer cappadocicum* 'Aureum', by contrast, just turns gold – but such a gold that the tree seems to be lit by brilliant sunlight. Other leaves, like *Koelreuteria paniculata*, turn blood-red. At the same time seed pods are ripening: the fruits of our native spindle are a dazzling mixture of orange and scarlet; the form *Euonymus cornutus quinquecornutus* has scarlet seeds winged with five turned-up points that look like jesters' caps.

The sensual year fades away in a miasma of fogs and damp. Leaves are slimy, crackling or leathery to the touch as we gather them together for the leaf-mould pile or the pungent bonfire, whose reluctant smoke scarcely rises above the ground. The autumn crocuses and colchicums fall apart. Acidantheras that have perfumed the air for so long are blown over by the fierce gales. Gardeners retreat to their greenhouses and firesides to make plans for next year, devising ways in which the garden can give even more sensuous pleasure.

FEW ASPECTS OF GARDENING have provoked as much discussion, in print and in conversation, as the use of colour. Colour circles (diagrams, not discussion groups) purport to tell us what colours go with what – and here begins the tyranny of good taste over those with little courage. Authors too seldom raise the question of what effect we want to produce, or what pleases us in a particular situation; we are given blanket instructions which, if strictly followed, would produce suffocating uniformity. Luckily gardeners are stubborn people, too practical and wise to listen to very much theory. And some gurus, notably Christopher Lloyd, having grown tired of conformist platitudes, are urging us to be bored by tasteful pastels and to go in for bold brash colours.

It is true that the qualities of any plant can be enhanced by what is put beside it. But which of its characteristics do you want to highlight? Its leaf shape, its flower, which may last only for ten days or so, the form of the flower, its habit of growth? Do you want to use contrast or harmony to achieve the emphasis? Take the beautiful euphorbia *E. charcacias* 'Lambrook Gold'. This is a stately evergreen which produces glorious golden bracts in spring; its emphatic form will make it the centrepiece of most plantings. What do you surround it with to bring out its finest characteristics? Possibly another euphorbia: *E. polychroma* grows into a low rounded dome and its yellow bracts are much brighter than Lambrook in full sunlight, although duller in the shade. The rounded shape will contrast well with the more upright Lambrook Gold, particularly if several polychromas are grouped together. But will the colour kill or enhance the Lambrook? That depends when they colour up and this will vary from year to year; perhaps polychroma will take over from Lambrook as it usually colours later. For contrast, another euphorbia, *E. griffithii* 'Fireglow' or 'Dixter', might be attractive, for its glowing, red bracts appear at much the same time; but this is a straggly plant and likely to run about out of control, so what about something smaller? *Anemone magellanica*, for example; this has the palest yellow flowers in spring which will not compete with Lambrook, but will deferentially echo and emphasize its colour. But the leaf shape of this plant is quite unlike Lambrook. Another solution is the lovely low-growing *Hypericum olympicum* 'Citrinum', which has the low rounded growth of *Euphorbia polychroma* but a much paler flower and tiny leaves. The problem is that it is often at its best after Lambrook has reached its peak. And so the search goes on.

It is fascinating to think in this way about a single plant and what to put near it; the search for perfection is never ending – which is why perhaps so many gardeners live so long; they are determined not to die before getting every plant in exactly the right place. But there isn't time to consider everything so deeply. And more often than not we are looking for an overall effect rather than perfection in a miniature composition. This may be achieved by repeating some lovely associations two or three times in the same border with variations between; this avoids the feeling of spotty over-excitement. A memorably beautiful long border in front of an old wall was composed in sections, with repeated plantings of *Potentilla fruticosa* 'Princess' and the rose 'Pink Grootendorst' to give shrubby backbone and divide it into segments. The colours were mostly muted pinks, smoky blues and silvers with some white galega and lychnis, the latter used for its silver leaves. There were repetitions in the herbaceous planting also – massive crambes foaming out at intervals and nepeta and diascia frequently emerging at the front to tumble out over the path. Once you have found an association that suits you, why not use it more than once?

Much over-elaborate colour theory could be replaced by the more important consideration of colour *tone*: in a carefully colour-coordinated border a tone that is too bright will ruin the effect unless all the colours are equally intense. The red border at The Priory, Kemerton, works so much better than that at Hidcote because care has been taken to select only the most intense tones. A yellow border which contains too much of the orange-yellow *Alstroemeria aurantiaca* (a very little will be too much once it starts to spread) is unbalanced by the intensity of this colour, which is as bright as the yolk of the freshest free-range egg. So merely grouping the same colours together won't do.

One of the most difficult colours of all to use is white. The white garden at Sissinghurst has exercised a pernicious influence, particularly inexplicable since it is not the most successful area of that glorious garden* (all those cardiocrinums formlessly flopping about over the tightly clipped box. And the box hedges too tall so that the visitor has to look over and down into the bed as into a grave). The problem with white is that it rushes forward to catch the eye before we can take in other colours; and this is particularly true of the purest whites, in phlox and the white Japanese anemones. The best white borders or gardens are those where great attention has been paid to the form of the plants, so that the border has architectural shape.

When some white phlox were moved into a particular border, in an attempt to lighten a patch of damp shade, the white completely distracted attention from the other more subdued colours. And something else happened; the lawn in front of this border seemed to change shape; it became less of an oblong and more of a square. This was a practical lesson in how colour can be used to change the shape of a garden. Some colours rush to hit the eye – whites, oranges and most strong, bright tones; others seem to draw the eye over longer distances, which is why they are often called recessive colours. Purples, mauves, lavenders and cool yellows are all recessive, as are most colours that are shadowy – again it is all a matter of tone.

How much you bother with flower colour is a matter of taste, but it is worth remembering that a wild-flower meadow, if you can find such a rarity, is full of colours that are coordinated by the growing conditions, not by any sensitive soul. True, the predominant colour is usually green and the flowers are dots against a green ground, but the mixture is rarely offensive. In fact, nature rarely offends, although it sometimes produces sports that are better eliminated. Take the barbarous *Caryopteris* called 'Worcester Gold', an unsightly mixture of powder-blue flowers and leaves that begin as lime-green and turn every kind of mucky shade between yellow and green, none of which does anything as background to the flowers. Why did anyone choose to propagate this form, which presumably turned up in a batch of seedlings, when the simple *Caryopteris* x *clandonensis* has the most lovely grey leaves which set off the flowers to perfection? It is much kinder to erase nature's mistakes than to perpetuate them. (Perhaps it is the quest for 'unusual plants' that is to blame.)*

Smells work on the human memory in a way that entirely bypasses the intellect; we can catch the faintest whiff and be at once transported back to somewhere we didn't even know we remembered. The most exciting smells in the garden ambush the visitor – we are suddenly surrounded by an unexpected smell whose source we can't detect. Or, as Francis Bacon put it so beautifully, 'The breath of flowers is far sweeter in the air (where it comes and goes like the warbling of music) than in the hand.' One part of the garden may be saturated with a smell, yet move two paces in the wrong direction and it is lost. The appley, astringent scent of the sweetbriar (*Rosa rubiginosa*) after rain is arrestingly powerful and so are phloxes later in the summer, with their peppery scent. Tiny plants underfoot, planted in cracks in the paving, spring their smells on us – thymes and the creeping mint, *Mentha requienii*, do this constantly. Because a powerful smell can stop us in our tracks, a scented plant can be carefully placed by a garden designer to make the visitor halt and so enjoy a visual composition which might otherwise have been missed. Scents hanging in the air around a seat conjure up ideas of medieval bowers and timeless lingering; if the seat itself is planted with thyme or camomile, our sitting down will make the scent rise. Dedicated planners for sensuous pleasure will plant *Thymus lanuginosus* on their seat because it not only smells but is silky to stroke – and is a lovely, lolloping name to say.

Other scents are more secret; you have to know which plants conceal them. The tiny leaves of the New Zealand mint, *Prostanthera cuneata*, are a glistening, shiny evergreen, but when crushed they give out a smell that blends peppermint with eucalyptus oil – the hotter the weather the more the latter smell predominates. *Pelargonium graveolens* has leaves smelling of lemon, sharply clean (water ice made with this is deliciously refreshing). Other leaves assault the nose less pleasantly: the lovely plant *Nectaroscordum bulgaricum* (formerly *Allium*), with cream and purple flowers, has leaves which smell of damp mackintoshes – an older generation says of gas masks. Flowers may similarly give a shock to the nose, delightful though they are to the eye. The hanging red tassels of *Ribes sanguineum* are a delight in spring, but keep them away from the path; can anyone enjoy the smell of cat that they emit? The deep red-purple spathes of the sinister *Dracunculus vulgaris* (another name to roll about the mouth) suggest this is no ordinary plant; the smell is not ordinary either – rotting beef, designed to attract the flies. Curiously, it grows hot in order to give off its powerful stink, and if you dare touch the shiny, dark central spadix you can feel its warmth.

Smells drifting in through an open window on a summer's evening remind us of idyllic days that seem reluctant to put themselves to bed, so lingering is the twilight. Wallflowers are perfect for this, as their name suggests, although they bloom early in the year, before the hottest weather. But climbers nodding in at a bedroom window in high summer give us a hint of paradise, and honeysuckles best of all. Bacon seems to have found their smell too strong, because he recommends them with the proviso 'that they be somewhat afar off'. Today the problem is to find a honeysuckle with a really good smell. Garden centre honeysuckles are never as fragrant as the labels proclaim and often simply do not smell at all. The best way to track a sweet one down is to sniff around the hedgerows on a summer's evening, or around an old country cottage with a tangle of climbers and birds' nests up to the eaves. Take or beg some cuttings from those and you will have captured a scent that will perfume your dreams for years to come.

Few things are more luxurious in winter than to bring a sprig or two from a sweetly scented shrub into the house – chimonanthus, Christmas box and, even more exotic in scent, *Daphne bholua* (some have thought it incense, others attar of roses). And of course the house may be sweetly scented from wood smoke, if we burn garden logs in the grate. Poplar wood takes ages to dry and then burns black with a sour smell. Conifer wood burns sullenly, but is deliciously tarry. But the dedicated sensualist will sit by his apple or pear wood, with a glass of tweedy malt whisky in his hand – the taste and the smell perfectly complementing each other.

Children touch things in the garden often and with pure pleasure – tree bark, rough grass, the prickles of conker cases, the soft petals of daisies; we pay less attention to the sense of touch as we become adult gardeners with tougher hands. But vegetable gardeners know well the delight of grubbing up the first cool, hard potato from the peaty tilth in which it is embedded – it comes up so clean and pure from the dark soil. Many tree trunks still invite us to touch them when we are grown up – the shiny, taut, red-brown bark of a *Prunus serrula* may be constantly polished by visitors' appreciative stroking, and the birches, particularly the white-trunked *B. utilis* and *jacquemontii*, have similar attractions. The deeply crevassed bark of an ancient walnut has precisely the opposite tactile appeal. Drawing catkins through the fingers gives the sensation of stroking rabbit's fur; pussy willow is like velvet on the back of the hand or stroked across the cheek. But some leaves are rewarding to touch because of their leathery solidity.

The contrast of the smooth, glossy sleekness of a mahogany conker rolled over and over in the palm with the damp, soft, moist inner lining of its spiny outer carapace, or the hairy stem of a poppy, felt before the indescribably soft, shiny inside of its petals – the sensuous gardener will find such subtle, tactile pleasures at every season. But it is necessary to separate out each delight and give it due attention if it is to be enjoyed to the full. A dazed sense of ecstasy does no justice to all the pleasures that gardening has to offer, any more than it does justice to any individual garden. As Thomas Traherne urged in *Centuries of Meditation*, we must learn to enjoy the world aright:

> *Your enjoyment of the World is never right, till you so esteem it, that everything in it, is more your treasure than a King's exchequer full of Silver and Gold. And that exchequer yours also in its place and service.*

CHAPTER NINE

THE MAGIC OF WATER, AN ELEMENT WHICH, OWING TO ITS CHANGEFULNESS OF FORM AND MOOD AND COLOUR AND TO THE VAST RANGE OF ITS EFFECTS, IS EVER THE PRINCIPAL SOURCE OF LANDSCAPE BEAUTY, AND HAS LIKE MUSIC A MYSTERIOUS INFLUENCE OVER THE MIND.

SIR GEORGE SITWELL
On the Making of Gardens

WATER

IN THE GROUNDS OF A CASTLE in the English Midlands is an excellent
garden with some particularly fine, deep herbaceous borders set in
front of the grey stone walls. Within the walls is an inner, courtyard
garden, with climbers massed luxuriantly and planting which foams
and cascades, restrained only by box hedging and paths. In high summer
it gives especial pleasure because so much is sweet smelling.

And yet, as you walk towards the heart of it, you feel a sense of
disappointment. There is an odd dullness. Something is missing.

Water.

The word occurs to you and at once you imagine it there, a still pool
reflecting the light upwards, and into whose depths you can gaze; or
water leaping up, to catch the sunlight and sparkle into fragments as it
falls down again to break the still, glassy surface. A single jet, carefully
placed, would do it. The garden does not call for anything in the way of
showy fountains – few private English gardens do; those look best either
in hot countries, or at least in great public parks and city squares.

But water brings life and light and movement, and acts as a focus.
Water lifts the spirits and helps to create *joie de vivre*, or else it soothes
and calms. It is full of life and draws other life to itself. Nothing

changes the garden more fundamentally, nor has such power to transform both the place and the mood of those within it. And the delight and satisfaction it gives are varied, and not level and constant – they increase. It is the most ancient and essential of garden pleasures. But it is more than a pleasure – there is something mystical and sacred about it.

In hot countries, where gardens have always been created as places of shade, solace and refreshment from the glare of the sun at noonday and the dust and dryness of busy public places, water was the essential feature; water that trickled sweetly over stones, sparkled and spurted effervescently, or lay in still, cool, deep pools. It was rare and prized, a precious balm to body and spirit.

Nothing is stiller than a dark pond, nor anything so absorbing. First the eye is drawn to the surface of the water, which reflects plants around the brim, the trees above it and sometimes the sky too. But after a time of sitting quietly and contemplating further, one's attention is drawn down to the intricate life going on below. The water, which had seemed so tranquil, is in fact full of activity. Below the water-boatmen skimming the surface, newts lie spreadeagled against the pond's sides, basking in the underwater sunlight; a frog rests its chin on a lily pad, winks slowly; goldfish nose out from under the plants to continue their patrol. The stresses and irritations of the day are soothed after half an hour of concentrating on this curious, busy and often predatory world.

In Chinese, the word for landscape is *shan shui*, which literally means mountains and water. And in Far Eastern gardens, water and rock are used constantly as small-scale reminders of the spiritually inspiring grandeur of the landscape. Suchow, the most famous city for gardens in China, lies on a flat plain, but the town gardens all have either a pool or a massive rock as the central feature of each courtyard, the former placed placidly horizontal, the latter thrustingly vertical. Each changes throughout the day with the alterations in the light, producing simultaneously a mood of peace and the interest of constant variety. Both rock and water were thought to have lessons to teach, though from the point of view of a very different culture we find those lessons difficult to understand.

The wise man delights in water, the good man delights in mountains.
For the wise move and the good stay still. The wise are happy but
the good secure

wrote Confucius, whose philosophy informed garden making as it did
every other aspect of Chinese life.

In some Japanese gardens, the stillness of water is replaced by the
stillness of gravel, which is raked into patterns which swirl around a
few, carefully placed rocks. Streams and pools created from pebbles are
seldom successful in other countries; our gardens are more literal, less
representational and symbolic. And we have no tradition of looking at
gardens as metaphors needing interpretation. Besides, we have so much
real water that seeking to imitate it in a material as rigid and hard as
stone merely seems perverse.

In one mood, still within a deep pool, water is placid, reflective, healing
to us; gushing exuberantly and frothily from a spout into a bowl, it is
invigorating; in its lively, generous moods, it reminds us of springs pouring
with wasteful luxury from Italian hillsides into mossed basins, and then
away into the parched countryside. The Roman writer Horace celebrated
a spring of this kind – his 'fons Bandusiae', more glittering than glass. In
less natural surroundings such waterfalls can be controlled in artful
shapes. In some of the greatest fountains, like Bernini's in the Piazza
Navona, the water is contrived to fall in what appears to be an unbroken
sheet of curving glass out of a thin aperture. In the Mogul gardens of
Kashmir, the water tumbles down a *chador*, a steep ramp with many small
steps in it, so that it chuckles and sparkles in its descent. Water here is
opulent and munificent. This was the characteristic the Persians, and
later the Arabs, celebrated in their paradise gardens; the four canals
meeting at a central point were a representation of the four great rivers
of the world and a celebration of all the life water brought with it.

It can be triumphant too, boastful and celebratory, reflecting not the
opulence of nature so much as the opulence of the garden's owner. The
supreme example is the Villa d'Este garden at Tivoli. Here, Pirro Ligorio,
working in the seventeenth century for Cardinal Ippolito d'Este, put
water through all its paces; it dances, spouts, spurts, sheets, up, down and
sideways. It accompanies you playfully down the handrails of the steps,

popping up every now and then like small, flickering lamp flames. It pours from a wall in a hundred spouts; it spurts from the breasts of stone sphinxes. At one time the water even played an organ; here its performance showed less virtuosity for, as Montaigne complained, 'the organ produced but one note!' If you decide to have water in your own garden – especially moving water – you cannot do better than visit the Villa d'Este and see what it can do. Go again after dark and see the effects achieved when moving water is lit; every plume of the fountain's spray sparkles against the black sky like an endless succession of fireworks.

In China and Britain, such brilliance is less often sought, less often achieved, perhaps because the sunlight in these countries is so much more watery and misty than the hard, brilliant sun of midsummer Spain or Italy. In Mediterranean countries the brilliance of water flung up to catch the sunlight against a background of dark yew or a line of sombre cypresses is unforgettable. Fountains need the sharpest of lighting. In the rain they seem absurd, not noble; their plumes of water dashing into the faces of passers-by in wind-blown Trafalgar Square merely irritate. There is also perhaps something in the national character of the British and the Chinese that rebels against anything so showy. In the eighteenth century, an age addicted to imitating what it was pleased to call 'Nature', Shenstone wrote that it was a sign of plebeian taste to have fountains in your garden. 'The fall of water is nature's province – only the vulgar citizen squirts up his rivulets into jettaux'; the scorn that fills that last foreign word shows how repugnant to him was the whole idea of a fountain.

Water plays upon the ears as well as appealing to our sight. At the Villa d'Este you will not only be dazzled but also deafened by the explosions of the great cascades. The tinkle of single drops falling into a ceramic container; the gurgle of water, as it bubbles up from a drilled stone or from the eddies created by a water chain; a chute with symmetrical, small barriers, curved like locks of hair, which make the water loop and swirl in its descent – there is a beautiful example at the Villa Lante. Or the constant but irregular crashing of a great fountain, hurling its water high into the air. In really hot climates the sound of water is often the most important feature of the whole garden. At Grasse, on a parched hillside in the South of France, the Vicomte de Noailles created a wonderful terraced garden full of rare plants. In his account of its creation he wrote, 'water is the life of a garden . . . the most important thing in my garden is the spring from the mountains. Some gardens are said to be perfumed. I would say this one sings.'

Water also has a soothing appeal to the sense of touch, which is why a pool raised to a height that is comfortable for sitting is such a delight. The sitter can trail a hand in the water while gazing into the depths, and the cool caress on the wrist is immediately relaxing and delightful. It is important that no one has to bend too far forwards to reach the water or the instability will revive the very tension that was to have been dispelled. And in any case, a formal pool that is not full – and full to the brim – is a monstrosity.

There are not many jokes in gardens. At Mount Stewart in Northern Ireland, Lady Londonderry's Red Hand of Ulster, planted in scarlet begonias, is a splendid exception. (Behind it, for those who concern themselves with political correctness, is an Irish harp shaped out of yew!) But water can lighten the mood; brooks are sometimes described as chuckling, and the sound of any running water, if not too strident, can be companionable, lively and entertaining. In the Renaissance gardens of Italy there were jets of water to ambush the visitor – no doubt to the infantile delight of the host. Seats and arches with hidden water jets would soak the breeches and the skirts of the unwary. Some gardens were even conceived as water theatres. Today we must be satisfied with fountains that dance to music, and with Disney's fascinating worm-shaped jets of water, which leap from one wire-mesh bed, arch through the air, and disappear into another. Both can cause an outburst of delighted laughter from spectators.

In England there are some great, celebratory water features, like the emperor fountain and the water staircase at Chatsworth, where there is even a water joke – a tree made of metal which spouts on to those who stand beneath. In hot cities like Barcelona, fountains have an essential role in public squares, where they refresh the stale city air and for a moment even dim the sound of the traffic. But in private English gardens, water is most successful when it is still, or moving with easy gentleness.

Lakes, with their dark mystery and perfect reflections, are a glory of formal English landscape gardens. The view across the one at Stourhead, to the neo-classical temple, is famous; but perhaps the most wonderful lake is in the secret garden at Stancombe Park in Gloucestershire. This is entirely hidden from the house, and from the visitor, who descends the steep slope through a bog garden, with its mysterious jungle of huge-leaved plants; and dives down into a grotto, the hectic descent leading apparently right into the earth. From this darkness one emerges to see the polished sheet of shining water which entirely fills the bottom of the valley. The lake seems enormous because the buildings around it, cottage, temple and boathouse, are so small. The jet-black surface of the water mirrors the sombre colour of a gigantic copper beech. This is a dream world, completely removed from familiar reality, a glorious demonstration of how water can give an entirely new and unexpected mood to a part of the garden.

On a smaller scale, Lawrence Johnston at Hidcote created his raised, circular pool in an enclosure of yew that is much too small for it. Here, the pool creates a mood that is different from that in any of the other garden rooms – mysterious and tranquil. This is a delightful piece of design, breaking all the 'rules' of proportion, but in the end a success we may all learn from. Water should always be a surprise, something given when we have no reason to expect it. This applies particularly to informal pools, which are a way of bringing the pleasures of a natural pond into the garden. They should be tucked away, in a glade, under the shadow of a tree, round a corner or behind a shrub mass where the visitor, suddenly catching sight of them, will gasp and stretch his eyes. In such a position, secluded from human intrusion, informal pools will soon become a focus for wildlife. Frogs and toads will breed there and, if they once discover they are happy in the pool, newts will return year after year, plodding with their serious gait across the lawn. Dragonflies will be heard rapping against the stems of tall plants and flashing their kingfisher-blue wings. In the evening birds will come to drink and in hot weather to give themselves showerbaths, particularly if you give them something, like a large stone or a landing stage, to stand on. This kind of pond is not hard to create and once it is in balance will not take very much time to keep clean. Some fish (grass carp are excellent) will act as hoovers, barley straw will keep the water free of blanketweed and oxygenating plants will freshen it. Even an annual clean-out can be immensely enjoyable; you will lift out the sludge of half-decayed leaves, covered in an oily purple film, and split up the water-lilies before they take over the surface, obliterating all of the reflections. If this is done on a warm spring day it is an engrossing task. Care has to be taken not to throw away any frog spawn or tiny newts which may be lying semi-dormant in the mud (leaving the sludge for a night beside the pond allows any creature which has been evicted by mistake the opportunity to slither its way home).

It is not easy to combine a wildlife pond with moving water, because the mud and slime in the bottom can clog up the outlet or the pump, but if you are lucky enough to have a garden where water occurs naturally, then a waterfall will be easy to create. If you cannot have sounds of water falling, then you must be content with the poppings and gurglings of the wildlife.

Formal pools, on the other hand, will be nearer the house, perhaps bringing light into a dark courtyard; here, a still pool reflecting the sky will have the brilliance of a mirror on even the dreariest winter day. A formal pool with a fountain might play outside a bedroom window.

The placing of water is important, particularly if you want your wildlife pond to look natural. It needs to be in a hollow or at the lowest point of the garden, but if the lowest point is not where you want it, it is possible to cheat by building up a supporting bank and then planting it with shrubs, so that the fall of ground on the other side of the pond is concealed. This is what has been done on a huge scale at Mount Stewart, the great garden in County Down. After the intricate pleasures of the Italian and Spanish gardens there, the visitor explores up a slope to find a hanging lake, supported by an immense dam, which is hard to make out because it is so densely planted. As one ascends, the reflections from the surface of the lake change in magical sequence, until the whole composition resolves itself and the distant towers of Tir na nog, the 'Land of the Ever Young', where the Londonderry family is buried, are seen among the trees of the far slope. The lake has inlets and mysterious hidden bays; it is partly planted round, but in places the lake's edge is left clear so that the water surface seems dark in places and bright in others. Humphry Repton wrote: 'Water on an eminence, or on the side of a hill, is among the most common errors of Mr Brown's followers.' But seeing the water on the slope above the garden at Mount Stewart makes one wonder if, in landscape gardening, there is such a thing as an error, in the absolute sense in which Repton uses the word. Can't all the rules sometimes be daringly and triumphantly broken?

Contemporary architects and landscape designers in many countries are as aware as ever of the delights of water and its versatility, and the charm it has for people who live, work and take recreation within sight of it. But the cost of really extravagant water features is now prohibitive and unless it is used brilliantly, it had perhaps better not be used at all. A cost-conscious, token bit of pool, puny little fountains, water that does nothing but lie, green and dismal in an uninteresting basin, is far worse than no water at all. No feature is more depressing when it goes wrong.

The very large pool or small lake of still water will be one of the most significant features in a garden. It catches the eye, draws the attention to itself and holds it there, so everything about it has to be considered extremely carefully. A dank small pond is unattractive. A large pool, not full to the very brim and perhaps with a mess of weeds, reeds and rushes sprouting around the perimeter like a week's growth of stubble, is extremely ugly. The edge of a pool can be very beautiful if left completely bare. If there is to be planting, it needs to be as meticulously planned as any border and even more meticulously tended. Reflections are important; tall slender trees, arching shrubs, pieces of stone statuary, need to be well chosen and sited with great care. A basic rule of physics is that the angle of incidence equals the angle of refraction – the line of sight will be bounced off the surface of the water at the same angle as it strikes it. So if you are placing a statue behind a pool you have to think where you want the whole reflection to be seen from and place it accordingly. The reflection of marginal planting can also affect the impression the pool creates; tall trees planted at the edge of the water will make it seem smaller and more mysterious, as the only light on the water's surface will be reflected from the sky. A pool with sloping banks always looks larger than one with vertical banks for similar reasons.

Water fenced off or netted over immediately loses its charm. Better to avoid having a pool altogether when children are small, or at least to use it as a sandpit until they are grown and then fill it with water when they are old enough to avoid its dangers. The sound of water can induce a feeling of irritability and restlessness too. A fountain placed in the courtyard of an old people's home, far from inducing a mood of relaxation, had the inhabitants constantly dashing to the lavatory. Pools which are too small can look mean and poky. We must think of the size of the pool itself in relation to the part of the garden it occupies. When you lay out the hose to indicate the placing and shape of the pool, you need to consider carefully whether it is the extent of the water or the extent of the whole construction which is being outlined.

Formal pools are usually best in formal, regular shapes, although in very modern gardens, where the main structures are free-form, the shape of the pool can become much more plastic. Informal wildlife pools usually look best if they take their shape from the ground form at the site. If a pool is not skilfully edged, the black butyl liner holding the water will be hideously visible.* Whenever such important details are ignored, water in the garden is robbed of its nobility, its opulence and its mirroring calm.

Before adding any water to your garden at all it is best to make a list of exactly what you require of it. Do you want still or moving water? If moving, will it gush out of a wall, or spout up into the air, or run gently down a stream bed? Is the effect to be formal or informal? Is there room in your garden for a mixture of both? It is usually a mistake to try to make the same piece of water fulfil too many functions. Consider the planting. Do you want it all round the margin, which may look messy and irritating, or clear lines where the water meets the land, with only the occasional arching shrub or carefully chosen tree reflected in the silver surface?

Of all the elements that may make up the garden, water can be the most moving, the most memorable, the most beautiful, the most profound in its effects. We were first at home within it, after all, so it is quite literally life-giving. Some gardens that have no water seem too energetic, with their foaming, sumptuous borders; they need the serenity and the restrained mystery that it brings. Others simply appear dull and dead. They need the liveliness of water and its reflections. Water can help to create whatever mood you wish – soothing and calming, leavening or invigorating, playful or reflective. But a garden without it is monotonous and impoverished.

Water is to a garden what an open fire is to a house. It brings life.

CHAPTER TEN

THERE IS THROUGHOUT NATURE
SOMETHING MOCKING; SOMETHING THAT LEADS US
ON AND ON, BUT ARRIVES NOWHERE; KEEPS NO FAITH
WITH US. ALL PROMISE OUTRUNS PERFORMANCE.

R. W. EMERSON
Nature

REVISIONS

GARDEN MAKERS ARE NEVER SATISFIED; there is always more to be done before the garden is finished. Next year that dead area in the shade behind the garage will be made interesting; next year the borders won't be allowed to die into drabness in August. Next year the ground elder will be tackled in a really systematic way. So plants are moved, bought, grown to achieve the next immediate objective, but there will be no end to the gardener's ambitions – nor his failure to achieve them. After the visions of imaginary gardens and the inspirations of the great garden writers comes the revision of our own garden, the attempt to make it something more like the ideal picture we have in mind.

Most gardeners are schizophrenics: half of the mind says the garden is lovely and they dwell in memory on the special days of beauty – familiarity breeding a kind of content; the other half makes them conscious of what could and should be done. Sometimes the errors and omissions are so glaring as to prod them into activity; sometimes a recurrent sense of unease suggests that all is not well with this or that part of the garden at this or that time of the year, but it is impossible to pinpoint exactly what is wrong.

Perhaps the garden is a new one, attached to a brand-new house and so only a 'garden' in name. Perhaps it is new to you: you bought it with the house and now that the interior decorating is complete it is time to consider the exterior. Perhaps it has long been yours, long been there – an unconsidered garden. But now you have become interested in gardens; you are beginning to be a gardener, and look at it with a critical eye.

And it is not right; it could be better, much better. You have been looking at gardens for some time now – good gardens, great gardens, rare gardens, charming, odd, interesting, pretty, awe-inspiring and altogether satisfying gardens. You are training your eye and learning to discriminate, developing your taste in plants, so that you choose one because it is pleasing and fitting for a particular place and not because it is 'plant of the month' at the garden centre. Now, when looking at your own garden, you see too much of what you do not like and not enough that you do.

So how should you begin?

You begin by doing nothing – except exercising patience, and this is the hardest part of all, because you long for your garden to be as good as you know it could be; you are driven mad every time you look at this, that, or the lack of the other.

Perhaps the best way of cultivating patience is to give in to *impatience* in a fairly controlled manner. Rip out a couple of dreary shrubs, dig the ground over and feed it; then go out and let yourself impulse-buy something you really do like, even if it's only a tray or two of instant, annual colour – deep azure-blue petunias or sweet-smelling stocks, or perhaps a pretty bush, a kolkwitzia just cascading into full flower, a *Lavatera thuringiaca* 'Rosea', which will give pleasure for the whole summer. Never mind if you eventually decide to do something quite different in that space, even to pave it over or set a birdbath on it. The annuals will die in the first autumn frosts and you can easily move the shrubs then too: people are far too nervous of moving things around in their gardens, but, provided you do it with care at the correct time, you can give your plants almost as peripatetic a life as the sofa and armchairs may enjoy indoors.*

But what if this radical action still leaves you less than satisfied?

Of course it may all be quite straightforward: the garden has outgrown itself – it is a mess. Right. An hour or two of careful looking, deciding and planning can be succeeded by a day or two of systematic hard work. That will soon put things right. But think first, and consult books and experienced gardening friends. Things may require hard pruning, but is this the right moment for it?* If you think a plant hideous, cannot bear to have it staring you in the face a moment longer, of course have it out. But before you do, consider if it is not merely in the wrong place. A tree often used as a focus of attention is Acer *pseudoplatanus* 'Brilliantissimum'. For much of the year this will disgust the eye with its leaves that look like wrung-out floor mops, but if you plant it in a less ostentatious position, where it can be enjoyed in spring when these same leaves are shrimp-pink as they unfurl from their striped buds, it is a delight. Later it will simply merge into the background among other trees.

Perhaps it is the whole composition that is causing unease, so that a radical reconsideration of the way you organize space in the garden is needed. Are the separate parts well proportioned? Is the garden's skeleton firm and clear? The English tendency is always to soften everything into a blur, so that the firm lines of walls, steps and kerbs lack definition. But almost all the great gardens have a firm structure: think of Sissinghurst with its clean lines of yew hedge, or the famous tapestry hedges at Hidcote which divide the garden into outdoor rooms. If the structure is wrong, then get on with the job of redefining the spaces at once; there is no time to be wasted.

But if you are satisfied with the structure, then ask yourself whether the lines of definition are of the right emphasis. Ropes swagged between posts with roses trained along them will define the limit of a space, but not as emphatically as a fence or a yew hedge. On the other hand some spaces may be oppressive because the walls are too definite: this can often be the case where a yew hedge has outgrown itself and put on a swaggering belly. Be fierce with such a hedge; prune it to the bone, one side at a time, and then feed it generously to show there is no malice in the severe surgery you are inflicting on it. (But don't subject all kinds of hedge to the same radical treatment; they will die.) By contrast, some spaces may need a lighter definition; pull up the dusty privet hedge and erect some trellis, then decide how many and what plants to grow up it; on this will depend the density of your wall.

With the spaces in the garden defined you might consider next whether there is enough mystery to lure the visitor on from one space to another. Or is too much given away at once? In some gardens the eye runs restlessly, all around, then away to the view, back to a waterfall, then to a seat, and finds rest nowhere: the garden has no centre, no focus. At the other extreme, if the garden is too mysterious, full of winding paths, shady glades and teasing glimpses, you may at one point decide to open it out to the distant view; a ha-ha will make it sweep out into the countryside, in breathtaking contrast to the confinement and control exercised elsewhere.

Something else that may irritate is the sense that the mood in some parts of the garden is not clearly defined at all; the distinction between spaces made for lingering and those for moving through is not clear. This may result in a vague feeling of dissatisfaction or unease – you don't feel quite happy sitting there, nor just passing through. At Sissinghurst (yes, again; it has become a standard by which we judge our gardens) this distinction is very clear; the garden spaces are ample, with many separated from each other by narrow yew corridors, which allow the mind and the eye repose before the next excitement. In your garden, do the places for lingering in feel welcoming? And are the seats placed as well as they could be? A seat set at random in an open meadow is usually an absurdity – it needs planting or a structure around it to give it permanence and presence.

Some borders are too much like fringes around the much-cosseted lawn; they skulk apologetically under the skirts of the hedges, as if too shy to draw attention to themselves by coming into the full light. These usually need either to be made wider, even if that means the sacrifice of some sacred lawn, or eliminated completely. Where the borders are too small the garden space may lack definition and thus a sense of permanence. A focal point may help to stabilize the whole composition, particularly if you feel it suffers from a spotty sense of disorder; maybe a tree, a fountain, an urn or a statue, or else a shrub of distinctive habit, such as *Viburnum plicatum* 'Mariesii' with its tiers of white blossom carried above the green leaves.

Sometimes the garden will seem all wrong because the shape of the site is intractable – too square or too flat or too narrow. But there are things that can be done to change the apparent proportions of the space, optical illusions to be created. Advancing and recessive colours can be used to make a square seem less regular; borders may converge at the end furthest from the house to make the garden seem longer – though if you do this, trees and hedges planted at the end of the garden must be kept small so that they too seem to be distant, or else the perspective illusion will be ruined. And flat sites can be modified: dig a pool or sunken garden and use the spoil from the hole to divide the garden with a raised walk.

Few gardens do not have dull areas or dull times of the year. Miss Jekyll coped with the latter by having plants in pots ready to plunge into the border, if the beauty of the composition began to flag.

Many gardens are dull in the winter and many gardeners have no desire whatsoever to have any dealings with them then. But if you do want late colour or scent, you can have them.

In August, gardens are often ragged and uninteresting and this is a much more critical time, because we are still outside a great deal. The roses and honeysuckle are over, but warm summer evenings can be made magical by the ghostly presence of white phlox, whose peppery scent hangs in the air. White flowers always seem to glow in the half-light of dusk. Japanese anemones (the whites in particular, 'Honorine Jobert', 'Whirlwind' and 'White Giant') signal the end of the summer holiday, and look wonderful planted with late-flowering scarlet fuchsia. The small annual *Lavatera trimestris* 'Mont Blanc', used carefully, will light up dreary corners and lift a bed that has gone over, and flower happily on until the first cold snap of autumn, when it will flush gently pink and give a different, quietly fading pleasure for several weeks. The heat of August suits South African plants too; a dignified and beautiful pairing at this time is blue agapanthus with the white, hanging bells of *Galtonia candicans*. *Thalictrum delavayi* and *Gaura lindheimeri* are also tall plants but with airy small flowers, the former like tiny pink powder puffs and the latter like red-and-white butterflies, and the gaura goes on flowering well into October. *Salvia patens** will need a warm spot but is worth any amount of trouble for its electric-blue flowers that appear in August. For the front of the border there is an increasing range of diascias to flop out over the path, with mats of pink and red flowers; they are not all hardy but the plant breeders seem to be making them more robust. The lovely deep purple form of *Origanum laevigatum*, called 'Hopley's' is charming on its own and even better planted against a background of grey foliage.

As the autumn sunlight thickens to a lemony milk and the first frosts are expected, the garden can still be interesting.* There will be a second, sparser flowering on the roses, and dahlias continue to be vibrant, but the great bulwark against winter is the Michaelmas daisies (Michaelmas is 29 September) – though they have two major drawbacks: they are martyrs to mildew and they flop all over the place if not staked. Three species are particularly valuable – *Aster frikartii* 'Mönch', which resists mildew, *A. lateriflorus* 'Horizontalis', with its haze of tiny purple and white flowers, and *A. thompsonii* 'Nanus', which can't flop because it grows to only eighteen inches. As to colour, the choice is enormous, but before you decide, visit one of the National Collection holders, such as Picton's Nursery, at Colwall in Worcestershire, in the middle of October and you will scarcely believe your eyes when you see the brilliant colours lighting up the gloomy days. Sedums too will prolong the garden's interest* and attract the late butterflies, and if you love lilies then plant nerines* in a warm spot with quick-draining soil; their pink, white or red trumpets are like miniature lilies. Another bulb for the end of the season is *Gladiolus callianthus* 'Murieliae' (it used to be called *Acidanthera*), with its sweet-smelling, dark-centred white flowers; (these will probably need lifting for the winter). Colchicums, often known as the autumn crocus, look best in rough grass, which gives some support to their naked necks. In borders, they fall about drunkenly and all too quickly collapse into pieces. Finally, if there is a slope in your garden to be made glorious late in the season, do not neglect the tumbler *Lespedeza thunbergii*. It has silky foliage and its deep red and purple flowers will add a daring splash of colour, to rival the blazing autumnal splendour of the trees.

Dead areas need to be tackled boldly. A dry bank in the sun might be covered in layers of gravel and stabilized with larger pieces of stone, to make it into a scree garden for alpines. In this way the characteristics of the site are turned to your advantage. Patches of dense shade can be lifted by the variegated ground elder, *Geranium macrorrhizum*, or *Cyclamen hederifolium* – one of the joys of September and October, making patches of white and pink even beneath a dense yew hedge and spreading rapidly where it is happy – or the annual self-seeder *Smyrnium perfoliatum*. You can cheer up the borders when they become dull by growing a late clematis through the foliage. Globed peonies are dazzling and opulent for a brief time but their glossy foliage persists for months after the flowers and a *texensis* clematis – 'Duchess of Albany', for example – will look like a late-flowering group of tulips as it holds its half-open blooms with their pointed petals above the peony leaves.

Is there anything about the planting of your garden in general that irritates? The thing to bear in mind is theme and variation, excitement and repose. If a particular combination pleases you, repeat it and perhaps vary the proportions of the constituent elements. If the border looks spotty then be bold again and have larger masses of your favourite plants. Finally, think about the structure of the planting, the architecture of its outline and the combination of leaf shapes within the whole. Flowers are only one small part of the plant.

There may be something about the hard landscaping that makes you uneasy – a set of steps that has no rhythm to it, so that you are always stumbling up and down them, or a wall where the pointing is so bad that the surface of the brick or stone is smeared unpleasantly with dried-on mortar. A path may have been badly laid so that it always turns into a series of pools after a shower of rain, encouraging the growth of slippery mosses.

And what if, after considering all these questions, you still find the garden vaguely depressing and lifeless, without any magic? Almost certainly what you need is some water, moving or still, the great transformer of a garden.

You have considered your garden and have begun to analyse what is wrong with it. What do you do now?

Once particular problems become clear, some of them at least can be solved simply by consulting the right books carefully. Then, in the course of an autumn and winter, when there is less to do outside, you can begin to make mistakes indoors, on paper, creating a series of plans and tearing them up again, compiling lists and crossing them out. This way, half a dozen styles and planting schemes can be tried and accepted, modified or rejected. The whole process is both educative and great fun – indeed, the whole business may be so enthralling that you will want to go a step further, and enrol for one of the many garden design courses springing up like mushrooms in many parts of the country.

Confidence comes quickly from looking and learning, before making plans and then the first tentative changes themselves. But however much advance work there may have been, the only true test is action in the garden itself, and if things do not look right after all, you can move them, make small adjustments, or have them out altogether and start again – very little is completely irrevocable.

Grand advice. But of course, any permanent structural changes and additions will have to be right straight away or much time, effort and money will be wasted.

It is easier to alter additions than subtractions – once a tree is felled there is no glueing it back into position, and it is quite a lot harder to visualize how a whole garden will look without a particular feature than with a new one. It is only by careful looking, spending time trying to picture how things will be from every aspect, that you can become surer of your judgement. If in doubt, don't – be prudent, wise, cautious: and boring. Look before you leap – but then do leap; don't dither, take a calculated risk. Otherwise you will never do the best for your garden, and it will remain a pleasant place but uninspired, unremarkable – dull.

Some tricks will help minimize the risk of serious errors. Supposing you want to divide the garden in some way, to shelter it more perhaps, or separate it into different areas; and plan to build a high wall, erect trellis on top of a low one, or put a solid gate in a gap. It is difficult to gauge the full effect this will have, no matter how many little sketches you draw, or how long you stand, squinting down the garden, so it may be worth buying some large sheets of cheap plywood, and trawling through builders' skips in the street for an old discarded door and mocking up the wall and door temporarily. It will not look good but it will indicate where the shadows fall and what sort of new spaces and enclosures will be created, and whether they are attractive or ugly. When you look at the new feature from the house, you may realize it is a mistake because it blocks some light or a particularly pleasing glimpse of a garden corner. Or a door may be exactly what is needed, but not a solid door; slice out some slats in the upper section and try that for effect, or cut the hardboard down to make a slightly lower wall, which may immediately look just right.

If you plan a garden pool and there are three possible sites for it, you can mock one up from industrial polythene sheeting or even heavy-gauge aluminium foil, beginning with a very large circle and perhaps altering the size, moving the 'pool' around, surrounding it with a circle of stones or bricks to anchor it. You can even stand a few annuals in pots around the edge to gauge the 'planted-up' effect. 'Paths' can be constructed out of sheets of card or even a row of paperback books. And it is amazing what garden structures can be 'mocked-up' out of the huge cardboard containers in which new washing machines and refrigerators are delivered.*

Once, few people had any alternative to making their own garden revisions: some rather grand garden designers did exist but they were inaccessible to ordinary mortals with modest plots and budgets to match. In any case, it would not have occurred to most gardeners to make use of designers; they grew things themselves and their gardens evolved gradually around what they grew. But in the last few years there has been a huge growth in the garden design industry; courses have proliferated and many people have taken them not only for their own interest, but perhaps after redundancy, or early retirement, or the departure of children from home, in the hope of making a new career and some income. Once, smart young women with cultivated taste worked in art galleries or auction houses before they set up in business as interior designers. Now, the latest fashion among them is for training in garden design (though rarely in practical horticulture). From being an invisible profession, garden designers have assumed a very high profile. If you want to make use of one there is a huge choice available.

Do you want to make use of one?

Some people have no use for anyone to advise them. In *Mansfield Park*, Edmund Bertram is absolute in his determination not to use what was then known as an 'improver': 'Had I a place to new-fashion, I should not put myself into the hands of an improver. I would rather have an inferior degree of beauty, of my own choice, and acquired progressively. I would rather abide by my own blunders than by his.'

Who can quarrel with these feelings? He wants to be his own man, expressing his own personality in the beauties of his garden, and he is prepared to wait, to change his mind, to approach the whole business in a tentative, thoughtful way.

And any client who really cares about the garden will want it to reflect his or her taste. Nothing is more depressing for a designer than to work for people who care so little about the garden that they will pronounce themselves delighted, whatever the proposed improvements.* It quickly becomes clear that they will not look after the garden once it has been made, because nothing of themselves has gone into its making. And how will they cope with its development if they have contributed nothing to the ideas that led to the design in the first place?

Is there then no use for a garden designer at all? Of course there may be. You may simply lack the inclination or the time to spend learning enough about garden planning to do the thing entirely yourself. But deciding whether you need a designer, and how to make the best use of one, requires much careful thought.

Someone coming to your garden with a fresh and experienced eye can help you to a view of its failings and possibilities quite quickly. An hour spent walking round, talking to a sensitive garden designer can change your focus, make you see what is familiar in a new and clearer way, and open your eyes, so that what you took to be the immutable data of the garden – the presence of a large ash tree, for example – suddenly become matters for debate. You are freed to see the place with new eyes and the experience may be intoxicating.

Or you may be thinking of extending the garden into an area that has so far been left uncultivated – part of an old paddock perhaps, or the site of a long-demolished outdoor privy, but have no idea where to begin. You may need advice on one specific project – the placing of a summer house or a pool, or the creation of a screen between you and the neighbours.

So you decide to use a garden designer. How do you find the right person? Before deciding whether a particular one suits you it is as well to make sure they have a basic qualification. It will not guarantee a great garden, or even one you can enjoy living with, but it should at least ensure a minimum standard of competence in essential matters such as designing pools, steps and walls which will be safe and durable, and you can be fairly confident that if you garden on very alkaline soil the designer will not fill your borders with camellias and azaleas, or set a row of poplars within twenty feet of your house drains. But qualifications will tell you nothing at all about a garden designer's taste and style. One way to begin is by choosing three or four likely candidates from advertisements in the specialist press or on recommendation, and first writing or telephoning for details of their charges, to make sure you can afford them. (Most will charge by the hour with a separate mileage fee, and will take a percentage of the cost of any contract, construction work or planting they oversee. An initial consultative visit is often free.)

Let's suppose that after some preliminary sifting you make three appointments; two men and a woman are coming to see you and your garden over the course of a week. That is very exciting. At last you feel you are getting somewhere.

Fred Ditching comes on Monday. He hands you a business card straight away and has a fat portfolio of photographs under his arm filled with pictures of driveways, walls, terraces and paving. Clearly, he is a hard landscaping man. He talks of where he will put your barbecue and patio and speaks a great deal of the relative merits of various kinds of stone and gravel. He tells you that your site is difficult because it slopes awkwardly, making it hard to work on it with machines, and suggests rather a lot of levelling. He admires some fine old trees but says they may have to come down. He asks about access for large diggers. He is an expert in his field, but his field is not design. He says little about the potential of the garden or about his vision of how it could develop. Plants are not mentioned at all, though he says he has an assistant who would do the turfing. Fred Ditching isn't the man for you, but the visit has not been wasted because you now know where to go when you need hard landscaping well done.

Amanda Beesnees is your Wednesday appointment. Her portfolio is thick with romantic photographs taken on misty, sunny evenings, of borders exuding good taste, whose colours are all pastel shades of pink, blue and silver grey. Other themes are repeated – enormous (and enormously expensive) containers, and rose arches everywhere. Her talk is of where you will put the water feature – did you know you wanted a water feature? She assumes you dislike dwarf conifer, most annuals, and anything orange, and that you adore hostas and hellebores and that trellis obelisks will make any garden elegant. You are uneasy. She seems to have a small set of fixed ideas which she will apply to any garden, merely shifting the combinations around a bit by way of change. She does not listen to what you are saying, if you dare to say anything in the face of someone who knows not only all the answers but all the questions too. If you employ her, might you not end up with a garden stamped, like an interior or an expensive garment, with its own unmistakable designer label, recognizable to anyone and referred to not as your garden but as 'an Amanda Beesnees garden'.

Friday brings Gervase Lithe-Swathely. By this time you are not feeling optimistic and are half tempted to cancel the appointment. His name makes you bristle. But as he gets out of his car he makes a comment on the entrance to the garden that at once changes your attitude. Here is someone with his eyes open, who notices the kinds of things that are important to you. Together you walk round the garden. He says little as you tell him some of the things you want it to contain. He looks beyond the fences to the surroundings, he pokes into odd corners, asks about the soil, the wind, the temperatures in winter. He makes one immediately sympathetic suggestion about cutting back some shrubs to reveal a small view. Then he wanders off by himself to get the feel of the place. And on his return asks you more specific questions about exactly what you want him to do. This sounds businesslike. In general you warm to him as a person and feel he may be someone whose knowledge and opinions you would trust. He seems to like the garden and thinks it has potential; he has made one or two warm remarks about it which make you feel less depressed at once, and pays you the compliment of assuming you are both interested and knowledgeable. Nor does he seem to have any rigid ideas which he wants to impose upon your garden; he hasn't redesigned it instantly for you, but says he needs plenty of time to think about it. So you ask him to do so and then to send some initial design ideas. It is only when he returns with these and explains them carefully, together with the reasons behind them, that you will know if he is someone you can work with.

There is no reason why all three designers should not be invited to draw up an initial plan – their vision of your garden, together with some suggestions for general revisions and improvements. You will have to pay for the designs, of course, but will be under no further obligation. You can study each of them and select the one you like best, or select the bits you like of each. It is rather the same, on a smaller scale, as being a public body, awarding the commission for a major new building after inviting entries from several architects. Take care when making your selection that you are not seduced by the beauty of the presentation. Garden design courses lay huge emphasis on it, often to the exclusion of the quality of the design, so look behind the pretty drawing to the ideas and see if they are coherent, persuasive and original.

Most garden owners will not want to be handed an impersonal, finished plan; they will want to be consulted, to work with and learn from their garden designer. Beware those who indicate that they do not welcome this. Beware the inflexible one who does not brook any alterations to the plan, cannot tolerate suggestions, or deals with them dismissively. Your idea may not be a good one – in that case, you need to be told the reason why. Is it simply impractical? Is there a basic rule of design or construction which says so? (There are very few of these: be suspicious of the designer who is ruled by them.) Or is it simply that your taste is considered naff? A good designer will try to lead you gently towards new ideas and possibilities for your garden, to open your eyes to plants you have not previously known of, or perhaps disregarded or despised, and to lure you away from some of the fixed ideas which are not helping you to do your garden justice.

When the designers present you with their plans they should be prepared to see them as a basis for discussion. First, they must be able to make them as clear to you as possible and help you to visualize what the reality might be like. Get them to walk over the garden with you, plan in hand, and talk it through at every stage. Ask any questions that you have to, no matter how stupid you are afraid they may be. Even if they are stupid, the designer should deal courteously with them. Particularly, ask questions about the garden in different seasons.

The designer should then go away and leave you to mull the plan over by yourself for a week or two, letting it sink in, digesting, making notes. You can compile a second list of queries, requests and opinions about the design – ideas for changes, important questions of estimated cost, and so on. Then ask the designer to come back and take the plan a stage further and discuss your thoughts with them. If their attitude is 'that's my plan for your garden, take it or leave it' and they seem reluctant to return unless to oversee the job as given, then leave it. Arrogance, masquerading as 'artistic temperament', is not helpful in someone whose profession involves dealing with people and their needs as well as with garden dreams and visions.

But in practice such characters are few, and you are more than likely to meet people who are interested in and enthusiastic about their work – gardens in general and yours, at least for the time being, in particular.

If you get along well with the designer, find that you are on the same wavelength and agree on general ideas and taste, and yet you do not find the design they have done for your garden appealing or attractive – it is simply not the sort of garden that you want or like – don't be afraid to say so. You do not have to accept it. Many people are shy of professionals, nervous of someone who appears to know a great deal: but *you* are the paying client, and provided you are courteous and give reasons for rejecting the design, there should be no ill-feeling on either side.

At this stage you may ask the designer to go back to the drawing board, or you may simply pay up and consult another designer at a later date. Never be bullied by someone into accepting a whole design, or aspects of it, about which you have any serious misgivings, and never let something go ahead about which you are unclear. Be prepared to make changes. With all the best planning and preparation in the world, things when completed can look very different from the picture you had of them. This is where you and your designer must have a friendly relationship, and an agreement that if necessary you will be bold and ruthless. Change it. Have it out. Be prepared to start again. This may be frustrating and time-consuming, but in the end you will both get the best possible garden. And it is the garden, your garden, which should be of paramount importance to both of you.

Are you a good client? That is what the garden designer is hoping for – he or she may like you, love your garden, and long to work on it ot make it beter. The job may be good in financial terms too. But the experience can still be made a frustrating and unhappy one by the garden owner's behaviour. Aside from the obvious rules – pay the bills promptly, keep appointments or rearrange them with plenty of notice – there are other considerations.

You change your mind. In one sense, that is your privilege. But the designer will be irritated if your reasons for doing so are not the right ones.

What are those? The best reason you can give for a change of heart is that you are still learning, perhaps very quickly: your knowledge is increasing, your tastes are forming under the influence of what you see and read, and so your vision of a good garden is developing too. What pleased you six months ago seems inadequate now. All good garden designers will accept this, even recognizing that they have been in the same situation. But to change your mind several times on a whim, and to ask for alterations simply because you have not bothered to study the design carefully or given any prior thought to your garden at all, is annoying.

Some changes may be trivial and easily accommodated: you suddenly develop an aversion to one particular plant – well, it may be replaced on a plan without much trouble. But if you ask for a border flowering very late in the season and featuring dramatic shapes and deep, vivid colours, only to decide it should comprise mainly soft drifts of understated pastels, at their best in early June, this will infuriate your designer. He has spent hours planning everything around a large pool as the focal point, even though your garden is not the ideal shape to accommodate it: you then decide, when construction is under way, to replace the pool with grass after all – imagine the designer's frustration. A bad client will be autocratic, dictatorial and thoughtless too: it is irritating if you don't explain that you dislike all roses, do not wish to have any trees and are planning to use an open rectangular area not as a velvet lawn on which nothing but a deckchair will ever be placed, but as a playing area for your adolescent sons. It is unfair to imply that you have £50,000 to spend on your garden when in reality your budget is extremely tight and you would be struggling to manage £2,000.

Consider your garden. Consider it as something to give pleasure and delight. Consider its importance to you. Consider your garden designer, whose vision and experience can help you to plan and revise and improve your garden. It will still be very much yours, yet will also achieve its full potential because of another person's eye and creative understanding.

This potential is sometimes revealed by natural disasters. A hurricane lays waste the shelter belt that should have protected the garden, or honey fungus quite suddenly kills a specimen tree which was an important focal point. At first you are inconsolable; the garden will never be the same. But slowly the ghosts of the dead trees fade and the

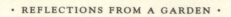

raw gaps become planting opportunities. Perhaps the shelter belt hid a wonderful view, which can be incorporated into the garden's new design. Perhaps the fine, old specimen tree was not in the very best place after all. So, in a spirit of hope and excitement a new vision of the garden emerges. Or this new vision may come about as a result of increased knowledge, new enthusiasm or altered taste. But all revisions should be fuelled by a spirit of courage and optimism.

EPILOGUE

THE SUNLIGHT ON THE GARDEN
HARDENS AND GROWS COLD,
WE CANNOT CAGE THE MINUTE
WITHIN ITS NETS OF GOLD.

LOUIS MACNEICE

EPILOGUE

ITIS EARLY EVENING. It is the beginning of July. There has been drama everywhere, these past weeks of high summer; drama on the lawns of Oxford and Cambridge colleges where students have played Shakespeare with the old stone walls for a backdrop. *The Tempest* and *As You Like It*, *Romeo and Juliet* and *Much Ado About Nothing* and, occasionally and more vociferously, brave performances of *Coriolanus*.

The Wind in the Willows is excitedly acted with squeaks and squeals among the laurels and rhododendron bushes of prep schools and *Alice in Wonderland* danced and *Oklahoma!* sung: whole villages worked for a year to mount the centenary pageant and grand opera has been sung in the grounds of quite modest country houses. Companies of optimistic young professionals have launched into tours, taking a minibus full of props and costumes to a dozen counties – *She Stoops to Conquer* alternates with *The Importance of Being Earnest*.

Ordinary people who work at desks and behind counters and wear unremarkable clothes – uniform blazers and practical cotton – are metamorphosed into strange, exotic creatures, slip into bright silk and enter other worlds. As the light changes trees darken, become denser and more mysterious, shrubs are no longer shrubs but furniture, walls, the ramparts of castles: the spaces between them lead to other worlds, beds and borders sink back into the dusk and disappear, white flowers emerge, ghostly pale. Anything may be about to happen. These open spaces belong to the Looking Glass world, to fairyland and magical kingdoms, to ancient Greece and to Illyria.

Gardens are not gardens now.

Every night this week the weather has been poor and the players unhappy, the audience damp and cold and stoical. The first night saw heavy scudding cloud and a little drizzle, the poorest light: on the next the wind blew, whistling eerily into the microphones and then veering, to blow the struggling voices clean away. Yesterday was hot and close and still until the evening, when the performance had begun and a thunderstorm cleared the air and the auditorium violently.

All over the country the story has been the same. Though that is no consolation.

But this evening, at last, it is perfect. All day the sun has shone and there has been the slightest, softest breeze. It has dropped now, leaving the air still and pure and sweet. People have relaxed, smiled, begun to anticipate. It is not too late, the enterprise not spoiled after all.

Six o'clock and still warm. The first cars are bumping over the ruts towards the field that is doing service as a car park. From here you cannot see the garden; there is a glimpse of the roof and stone chimneys of the house, behind a belt of beech trees. Otherwise, once you are out of the field that is the car park, there is a path across another area of rough grass towards an opening in a long, high hedge, a good sort of country hedge, left to grow as it pleases, all out of shape: it is densely green now, but in spring will be curded white with clots of blossom from March to May, blackthorn and hawthorn, wild damson, wild cherry, wild plum.

The gate in the gap stands open, inviting. Those who are going to picnic before the play are arriving now, babies as well as provisions carried in baskets and little children running ahead towards the mystery lying beyond the hedge, the elderly more cautious over the uneven ground.

A theatre. A stage. An auditorium. This is a private garden not usually open and never before for a play; no one knows what to expect. And at first they find nothing, going through the gap in the high hedge, nothing but another hedge, with a dark and narrow path leading to left and right. Which way? The children run, hesitate. Run back. Which way?

Come this way then, take the left-hand path along the line of the inner hedge, led on not by sight or sound but by scent, the smell of philadelphus and honeysuckle and the last of the roses. Only a little way and around a corner. But no, this is not the theatre, not the play. It is a garden, an inner room. Quite empty though, so that coming into it people hesitate, uncertain. But then move forward with a feeling of quiet pleasure. It is enclosed on four sides by the hedges, but these are of yew now, clipped smooth and straight. There are no flowers, no beds, no bushes, only close-mown grass and a rectangle of water, shallow in its stone channel, dark and still with half a dozen flat water-lilies outspread, their petals pale as the moon.

Which way? Which way? There seems to be no way. But of course the children find it, a slit in the hedge, guarded by a single great, grey urn. And now from somewhere ahead, a chink of glasses, crates being set down and voices echoing oddly. Steps, wide, semi-circular, comfortably set, lead down into a sunken avenue between great beds of scent. This is where the philadelphus and the honeysuckle, the roses and the lilies grow, tall and thick, knotted and swagged together, over walls and arches and trellis, around pillars and posts, with catmint and lavender trailing out across the path, studded with bees. And at the far end more steps leading up again and a great spreading cedar tree seen through an arch in the wall. Up the steps. Is this the end? Is it here? The baby and the basket are heavy. The elderly suddenly tired.

Through the arch.

And there it is, ahead, and all round – the garden. There *is* a garden. Only it is not just a garden now. Tonight, it is the theatre.

The grass stage is before an embracing semi-circle of high shrubs, rhododendrons and azaleas, with laurels behind, the flowers long since over, leaves densest, darkest green. There are seats on benches and on ground sheets, with supplementary chairs ranged around the edge and places to picnic, a ticket hut, an awning over the bar.

It is very warm, the air scented and still. The leaves do not stir. The shadows are lengthening, darkening and sharpening, hard edges cut across the grass. The garden forms a protective shelter around the audience and empty stage, tall trees on the outer circle, poplars and limes, metasequoia and cedar and one or two great oaks. Here and there, paths lead out of sight interestingly behind hedges, to where voices murmur, actors prepare. Tonight the garden will work its magic on them and they sense it, changing as best they may, cramped behind sheds and shrubs in makeshift dressing rooms. They had almost lost heart, weary of battling against wind and rain and audiences made restless with discomfort. But tonight all is well and will be well, there is an edge of excitement as the people come in through the arch and fan out across the auditorium, eat and drink and anticipate, find their seats, spread their rugs and cushions. The sun begins to drop a little behind the great cedar and deepens at the heart, red-gold. The scents of the flowers and the new-mown grass intensify on the evening air (though the gardener does not approve but stands somewhere, not quite out of sight, fearing the worst. It is not natural for a garden to become a theatre).

Little by little the sun slips down, the light changes, changes again: the picnics are packed; people begin to settle. The sky is the colour of a thrush's egg, damson at the rim, enamelled, brittle. And then the other lights come up, concealed in bushes, and at once the garden really is a theatre and the lawn a stage, the shrubs and trees recede into blackness and become wood, cardboard, inanimate. Music weaves in and out, and vying with the music every thrush and blackbird in the county madly singing.

There is drama already even before the play has begun and the people are part of it. The dramatic features of the garden are accentuated, shapes and masses become important, light and shade alter the atmosphere: white flowers become ghostly, there are secrets just out of sight, a gate may open unexpectedly, a path lead anywhere. At this time of the evening things are glimpsed out of the corner of the eye, quick movements; someone looking left towards a gap in the bushes sees a line of strange figures in costume, orderly, quiet. Preparing to come on, exotic people in scarlet and lemon-yellow and brilliant pink are transformed by golden coronets and animal heads and huge wings. The sight brings a shiver: for a second it is not like being in a garden or even in a theatre; it is like being in a dream, when the ordinary place is no longer ordinary and people are unrecognizable; it is a surreal world, garden, theatre, fantasy.

Little by little the light is seeping out of the sky, the sun is slipping down. And then the moon sails up and seems to rest at anchor, high over the cedar tree. The audience rustles and settles to silence. This moment is caught and held, everything comes together, poised, expectant. People are suddenly very conscious of the garden that lies all around them and holds them within itself, at the last moment before it is quite transformed.

A fanfare, a flourish and suddenly the empty space on the lawn is full of bright colours and movement as actors emerge laughing, talking, in procession from among the dark bushes. We are at the palace of the Duke of Athens.

'Now, fair Hippolyta . . .'

For three hours then the garden is forgotten, a background only and soon so dark it might not be there at all save that now and again the smell of the flowers drifts faintly across the grass from the sunken avenue.

The play proceeds, now tender, now bold, provoking fits of laughter, moments of silence, tears. Child actors in ears and tails and gauze flit and leap, strut and dance and every word spoken falls clear and sharp as a stone on to the air.

In the wings, which in life are the rhododendrons, the director smiles a beatific smile and folds his arms and basks in the absolute perfection of the moment. For it is as he dreamed in his fairest, wildest dreams: everything has come together, actors, words, music, light, sound and the magical garden. It is the result of hard work and forethought, careful planning, and inspiration too. And chance, the accidental coming together of every element, in right proportions, at the right time. Chance. Yes. He knows it very well, and that it was not within his directorial power to control the weather. But, just for this one, prideful moment, he believes it might have been. And so dreams on now, of a stage set in the middle of a great lake, perhaps, fireworks, an orchestra, *The Tempest*, magical effects . . .

But there is magic enough here in the garden, which is so much more than a garden and better than any theatre for this one night. The stage is empty and dark until a single spotlight falls on to the grass and into it, from nowhere, springs Puck, a streak of silver, half sexless child, half sprite, and darts from end to end followed everywhere by the light, brushing imaginary cobwebs from hydrangea and azalea and laurel bush, before standing utterly still to bid goodnight and seek applause and vanish in an instant, leaving the light a mere pinprick upon the ground.

For a long moment and several moments more no one stirs or speaks, reluctant to be the first to break the spell and the babies sleep in their baskets and children lying across laps and parents touch hands as lovers again and the elderly smile and smile. But then, one by one, people begin to stir. The applause begins, rises and breaks like a wave over the actors, blinking and smiling in the spotlight. People begin to move cramped limbs, to murmur, to come to and find themselves, after all, back in the garden where a little damp is beginning to rise from the grass.

Across the lawn, out of the theatre, under the arch and up the scented avenue towards the steps. In the still pool in the heart of the secret garden the water-lilies are closed now and only the face of the moon lies upside-down on the water. The box smells pungent, holding the warmth of the day and some faint memory of the past within itself. There is a long, slow, tired trail of people to the car park field, and in the garden, for a moment, clearing up and tidying, shouting and joking in relief and the mood is broken and ordinary, the garden and the play are pushed to one side, to be recalled later when the tales are told. The rest of the tidying and clearing will be done, dully, tomorrow.

And in an hour they are all gone. The garden settles back into itself and a breeze sneaks out of the bushes and over the grass. Later it will be cooler, later the clouds will gather and thicken so that by dawn it will rain, for this has been a poor summer and tonight a rare and precious interlude.

Now the sky is clear and there are stars, and the moon is full and pale and beautiful over the lawn that was the stage and the garden that was a theatre, a changed and magical place. But now is only a garden, after all.

AUTOBIOGRAPHIES

Susan Hill

I HAD NO GARDEN I COULD CALL MY OWN until I was in my thirties. The gardens of my childhood grew first in books, or else they belonged to other people.

We lived in Scarborough, a resort on the north-east coast of Yorkshire, town of high, handsome houses, sweeping avenues and crescents and a very great many gardens. And, in my childhood, during the years immediately after the war, it was also a place of a great many elderly people living in genteel, reduced circumstances in large, gloomy Victorian villas or the flats converted out of them. The gardens of these houses were relicts from Victorian and Edwardian England too; there were a great many gloomy old shrubberies and a lot of laurel, yards of high privet hedges in which little wrought-iron front gates were set. It was when I was gate height that I stood and gazed through them on all our walks between home and school, shops and bus stops. I was haunted by some of them and sometimes frightened too, by dark tunnels of yew, overhanging bushes, nooks and crannies – it was secretly, wonderfully alarming and I have never completely got over my unease in certain types of garden, among dense bushes and high hedges, especially alone or at dusk. I want my gardens to induce such feelings in me, need them to have secret and slightly disturbing corners. I was like Alice, peering down the dark passage towards the brightness and the growing things; for there were usually flower beds full of those bright, formal flowers and, in spring, thousands of snowdrops and crocuses in circles under ancient garden trees, often coming up through the snow which lay over Yorkshire for many of the weeks from January to March.

Two gardens in particular were desirable and fascinating because I was not allowed in them, and because they were guarded by witches.

The first witch occupied the ground-floor flat of the tall gaunt house in whose attic rooms we lived. She owned the house and hers was the garden. None of the other tenants had right of access and especially not a child, who might cause damage and disruption and make an unseemly noise beneath the witch's windows. I never would have done. I was a silent child, preoccupied with my inner imaginings. And once or twice, after I had been ill and the doctor had ordered plenty of fresh air, my mother succeeded in getting permission for me to walk quietly about in that garden, during the afternoon. Quite what damage I might ever have done there I am at a loss to know, for there was precious little to be spoiled – a square of grass and a privet hedge bordering the path on one side, a low wall on the street side with a couple of mangy flower beds. In these grew a great many London Pride and some enormous, prehistoric, gnarled irises, with vivid, waxen tulips in the spring. But I did not mind. The purple-blue of the irises was a magic colour to me – it still is – and I held long conversations with the London Pride and walked solemnly round and round the grass. Once, I stepped on a flower bed by accident and immediately there was such a rapping on the bay window that overhung it as caused my heart to leap. The witch had been watching me, as she always did, standing there ready to bang with her walking stick, her glasses glinting. I was terrified of her. I did not even dare to pick the daisies to make a chain. I went into that garden so rarely and there was so little, yet I knew it so well and loved every inch of it.

The other garden was even more beckoning, the stuff of dreams and wild fantasies, infinitely desirable. It lay on the other side of the high wall that bounded the next-door house, a grey, Scottish baronial-style mansion, with wide entrance gates set between stone pillars and a sweeping gravelled drive.

A witch lived here too, last survivor of a large and once rather grand Victorian family. The dark-green plush curtains were barely apart and great aspidistras and palms excluded what little was left of the light otherwise. I never saw the witch. No one did. But that she *was* a witch I was in no doubt. I wonder why so many of the old and lonely were hostile to young children then: perhaps because they had had very little ever to do with them. We were odd, alien creatures, a breed of young savages – even a quiet, solitary little convent school child. But that garden was beautiful to me, though in a very different way from those full of the bright flower beds. It was very formal, with a curved yew hedge surrounding a circular lawn, out of which niches for Italianate statues were cut, and in the centre was a fountain spurting from a stone basin. I recall no flowers there, except for some white roses climbing over a trellis, and a mass of snowdrops in February. But there was a greenhouse, very large and running along the side wall of the house, and in here, when he was not mowing the grass or clipping the hedge, the gardener worked, among a mass of potted plants: goodness knows what or who they were for – himself, I suppose, for I never saw the witch in either hothouse or garden. The gardener bore every resemblance to Beatrix Potter's Mr McGregor, sour and snarling. My attic bedroom overlooked the austere, dark-green garden and I used to stand staring down into it, wanting to be there, wondering, speculating. It is surprising that it had such appeal. Perhaps if I had been free to go through the gates and spend as much time as I liked, it would, like all mysterious places, have lost its charm.

There were other gardens I gazed into as we walked around Scarborough, and once we went to London and there was a garden there too, behind padlocked gates, with a sign that read, 'PRIVATE. RESIDENTS OF THE SQUARE ONLY.' Garden owners are generally so welcoming now, in the days of the Yellow Book, but they did not seem to be in the 1940s and 50s.

But there were public gardens in plenty to make up for it. Scarborough, like most seaside resorts, was a proud part of that great municipal tradition, then still in its heyday. Some gardens seemed to have been carved out of the cliff face itself, and yet behind their screens of trees were often as sheltered as any in Torquay or Bournemouth. The

Italian garden, the scented gardens for the blind, the rose gardens – I walked down and climbed back up the steep paths to them all, day after day, and played among steps and statues, flower beds and fountains, while my mother sat on a bench, reading, knitting, chatting to her friends; I marvelled at the floral clock and at the Shuttleworth miniature garden, which had a tiny boat tied up beside a little stone bridge, a model summerhouse a foot high, alpines for trees and bushes, and felt as a giant among the Lilliputians. But 'NO ENTRY' it said. 'KEEP OUT'. Look, do not touch. You were not allowed to clamber over the little box hedge. Another secret world, teasing the imagination, another forbidden garden. I suppose I must have believed, during those years, that they always belonged either to witches, who would cast a spell on children who stepped on the grass, to the Parks Department, who could put you in prison, or at the very least to the gardeners themselves, who would chase you out, 'waving a rake and calling out, "Stop, thief!"' Owners did not seem to garden then – gardeners did, just as grocers groced and bus conductors conducted.

My school had gardens and they were rather odd too. It was a convent and the garden was a large square, enclosed by the buildings on all sides. There were many beds of bright flowers – the scent of wallflowers in the hot sun brings lessons and classrooms, chalk and scratchy brown uniform back to me in that extraordinarily vivid way in which only smells can restore the past. There were a lot of huge lilacs and some wonderful sweet-smelling philadelphus. But peculiarly, there were also hideous stone grottoes built to house statues of the Virgin Mary, a cage of canaries and another of chickens, kept by the sisters, and a path leading to the Community garden, where silence reigned and nuns walked round and round like black crows, saying their beads – and we were forbidden to enter, or walk among the shady trees and look down into the gleaming lily pool.

And then it was over: paradise lay behind me as my family moved to the industrial Midlands. No sea. No public gardens, it seemed, only the 'landscaped' grass below the blocks of brave new flats. Gardens belonged to a world that was gone, to the mysterious imaginings of childhood and between the pages of books.

I did not have a garden of my own until nearly twenty years later, when I moved into a small Victorian terraced house in Stratford-upon-Avon, which had a long narrow walled garden, already so well established with climbing roses, swags of honeysuckle, a great white lilac and numerous mature shrubs, that there was little scope to do more than sling a hammock between the two old pear trees and enjoy the hot summers of 1975 and '76. I only began to tend a garden on moving to a cottage in a village near Oxford, five years and a daughter later. The garden faced north and east and was so windswept that everything was at least three weeks late coming on and things over two feet high were blown down unless I staked them. I put in a mass of white and pale pink peonies and several old varieties of apple on dwarf rooting stock. But otherwise I kept chickens and concentrated on vegetables and wrote a book about a year lived under our Magic Apple Tree there; the flower garden was more or less left to take care of itself. I would have liked to do more, but I knew nothing at all about how to design or properly plan a garden. I only knew what plants I did not like – and there seemed to be an awful lot of those. So, nervously, I retreated back to potatoes.

My gardening has changed dramatically since then though. I garden on another windswept site – it blows a gale from the west and sometimes, piercingly, downhill from the north-east on to the eighteenth-century stone farmhouse in the north Cotswolds where I have lived since 1992, a couple of miles from Lawrence Johnston's great garden at Hidcote.

Once, there was a stone wall around the front garden, within which were apple and plum trees and a yew arch, and cabbages grew among the roses, and lavender lined the path up to the front door. But when the cowsheds went, twenty-odd years ago, the garden was razed too – even the wall came down, and four and a half acres were laid to grass dotted with some unsuitably suburban sapling trees. Vandalism? Yes; but there is a lot to be said for inheriting a *tabula rasa*. In the four and half acres, plus another thirty of what are at the moment still fields, I am trying to make a new garden with Rory Stuart's expert help and vision. It is at least a twenty-year plan but we have done much already, from planting a cherry orchard to making a lake. The excitement of watching it take place, seeing bulbs emerge, trees grow and come into leaf for the first time, plants settle down and flower and become gradually established, is very great, and I am learning all the time, catching up fast on knowledge, developing and honing my own taste. My ideas are becoming clear and definite, and very personal indeed. I dislike fussiness, like very few plants and hate most colours.

But above all I should like the garden to have something of the mysterious appeal and secret strangeness of those gardens of my childhood. But here, though there may be dark corners and hidden delights, there will never be signs saying PRIVATE, NO ENTRY, and KEEP OFF THE GRASS, never be a witch at the window to frighten away children, never be a Mr McGregor, employed to wave a rake at a young rabbit, surprised among the lettuces on a summer morning.

RORY STUART

I WAS NO CHILDHOOD GARDENER. There was no small patch of earth tended with fierce devotion and planted with marigolds and hollyhocks. It all started much later, when I was left a beautiful garden by my plantswoman aunt, Nancy Saunders. She was an expert botanist who collected plants from all over the world and imported them in her sponge bag (quite legally, with a licence) to her Gloucestershire garden. On frequent stays I admired the beauty of the garden she had made, but never asked what made the garden beautiful. Nor was I more alert in learning the names of plants; Nancy would make me learn one name each time I came to stay and I was tested on my next visit. I always failed.

Such an unpromising start hardly fitted me to take care of such a collection of plants after my aunt's death. I was a part-time inhabitant of the house, so the garden received only sporadic attention, consisting for the most part of weeding and tidying up the borders. I wince now when I think of all the treasures which were hauled out because of my ignorant inability to distinguish between weed and rarity. At this stage the garden was a burden. Then I decided to plant something. This was a great step forward because it meant I was changing the garden rather than attending it like a museum keeper. My first plant was a *Hydrangea petiolaris*. It had to go in a place where no plant had previously grown; I hadn't yet the courage to oust any of Nancy's plants. So, poor thing, it was tucked into an unpromising dark corner very close to the house wall, where for years it sulked; finally it decided to grow and is now a giant requiring annual pruning.

I didn't realize it at the time, but this planting was the start of a new interest which was to change my life. Wondering what else I might plant I started to read about gardens and gardening. Kind friends came to stay, taught me names, helped with the weeding, guided my threatening hand away from rare and interesting plants, suggested new things to plant and gave me cuttings. I began to visit gardens. And to look with opening eyes. Visits to gardens suggested new ideas and provided the opportunity of testing the memory to see which plant names had stuck. An interest was becoming an obsession.

More and more new plants were added to the garden. Some flourished under the regime of benign semi-neglect, others failed. It was only after murdering five romneyas that I got one to grow. Some of Nancy's original trees died of honey fungus. At first their loss seemed unbearable, but after about three months the gaping hole miraculously transformed itself into a planting opportunity. My aunt loved so many trees she inevitably planted them too close together, so some thinning out was needed and this gave me the chance to plant new trees – much too close together, as I am now beginning to realize. Trusting friends began to ask advice on their gardens, which made me realize how little I knew about what I later learned to call 'hard landscaping' – steps, paths, walls and so forth – at which point a professional garden design training seemed a good idea. And thus an interest became a way of life. Like my now-established romneya, an interest in gardens is invasive. It throws up suckers in unexpected places; I find myself lecturing on gardens, writing about gardens, taking tours of gardens, photographing gardens and designing gardens. All of which gives rise to a new dilemma. The more work of this kind I have, the less time there is to look after my own garden. Where will it all end?

GRUMBLING
APPENDIX

U P TO THIS POINT, *Reflections from a Garden* has been written as if by one person, using a single authorial voice.

We have collaborated most amicably, spent hours in detailed discussion and agreed on much – the book has not been divided up and separately apportioned.

But in fact, two quite independent and strong-minded people, often with distinct views and differing opinions, have been at work; we have disagreed, sometimes mildly, occasionally vociferously, and where would be the point in disguising the fact? Rather than trying to talk each other round (a fruitless exercise), or to present a bland surface of compromise, we decided to separate and reveal our differences.

PRELUDE

*Why is there a photograph of such an ugly summer house, such a disproportionately large urn, such a wearisome length of yew hedge? To serve as warnings (page 3).

Does anyone take a photograph of something ugly as a warning? More often it seemed beautiful or remarkable at the time but later you can't think why. R.

VISIONS

*. . . *as we grow up and become gardeners we may have a sneaking sympathy for Mr McGregor* (page 18).

Nothing sneaking about it. The constant battle against small, furry creatures with insatiable appetites makes the gardener's sympathy whole-hearted. This is just one of the ways in which the gardener is at perpetual war with nature. R.

We are as much lords of these parks, grounds, gardens and messuages as the noble inhabitants (page 26).

If, that is, we can bear beyond page 10 the company and vacuous conversations of such feather-headed idiots, and no plot other than the endless ditherings of nincompoops. R.

BEGINNINGS

* *'What are kept in ironmongers shops as "ladies tools" with varnished handles and blue blades and that are usually given to children, are wretched things – badly shaped, badly balanced and generally weak where they should be strongest'* (page 34).

This is still true. Manufacturers produce children's gardening tools which twist, bend, break and snag the fingers. What could be more frustrating for the infant gardeners? Enough to put them off gardening for life. R.

*. . . *the . . . ornamental vegetable gardens, which it is* de rigueur *to call potagers* (page 37).

The pursuit of fashion often pretentiously cloaks itself in foreign vocabulary to make the simple and familiar sound new and exotic. The word 'potager' means a kitchen garden. R.

The vision of your own perfect garden will still be hazy in detail. But nevertheless it will lead you on like a star (page 44).

This star may shine clearly at first, but later on in our gardening lives the vision becomes more of a mirage. R.

VISITING

Blades are this man's pride (page 50).

Yes, it is usually the male who gardens like this, the standard of perfection perhaps being set by the closeness of his morning shave. In some partnerships, of course, this trim-back-and-sides gardening is the only sort that she will permit. R.

LIBERATION

If you really rather like having daisies and speedwell on your lawn and are happy to put up with a little seasonal shagginess about the edges, you will save yourself a great deal of work and worry (page 64).

Not just this, you will make your garden more restful to be in. Perfection in garden art is never restful, perhaps because we are always naggingly aware of how temporary is such an ideal state. In this, garden making differs from other arts: perfection of musical phrase or sculpted form is elevating and confers a kind of repose on the spirit. R.

If you do grow vegetables, it ought to be self-evident that you are perfectly free to grow only the ones you actually enjoy eating (page 66).

Isn't it? R.

So more moments of liberation come when it dawns on you that you do not have to grow any vegetable you don't actually like (page 66).

Is this gardener mentally challenged? It seems to have taken him or her an inordinate amount of time to reach the obvious conclusion that you can grow what you like in your own garden. R.

DRAMA

. . . or a ravishing smell hanging in the air, often exuded by leaves as we gently stroke them (page 75).

Not enough plant names here. OK: rosemary, catmint, thyme, *Prostanthera cuneata* (the New Zealand mint, but actually it smells of eucalyptus and has white flowers, shaped rather like a salvia), and *Houttuynia cordata*, whose leaves smell of burnt oranges when crushed. R.

* . . . our secret place might be a tented enclosure created by the boughs of . . . a weeping silver pear (page 76).

That's fine if the weeping silver pears are going to be pruned like umbrellas. Otherwise I wouldn't want to try crawling under one and sitting curled up uncomfortably with trailing branches getting in my ears and hair. s.

* The pleasures of eating in the open are undisputed (page 76).

Well, I dispute them. I hate picnics. They are never so idyllic. They are wasp- and beetle-ridden and soil and grass keep getting into the food. s.

* Laid lengthways along a path, the effect is to hurry the walker to the end (page 82).

Or to his end, which is the impression created at Tottenham Court Road Underground Station. The frenetic commuters must be maddened still more by the pattern of the bricks in the pedestrian tunnels. R.

* At Painswick House in Gloucestershire there is an extraordinary piece of garden drama, where expectation is wittily disappointed (page 83).

I couldn't disagree more about this garden feature. I find it an absolutely lost opportunity. We should go through the door and at once the whole garden should be revealed breathtakingly, laid at our feet so that we are stunned by it. There should be a slight sense of vertigo too, and then a path, visible immediately, leading us down into the garden. As it is, you never get the full impact – by the time you are down one of the side paths, you are on a level with the garden and an opportunity has been lost. A most frustrating place. A dramatic effect should not be despised just because it is obvious. s.

TIME

*If a garden could be preserved at a moment of perfection and therefore set outside of time, it would become an embalmed garden, lifeless, and pointless as silk flowers (page 90).

Susan would not let me include Keat's sensuous lines which exactly pinpoint how the ecstasy of pleasure depends on our perception that it is transitory. So here they are:

> Ay, in the very temple of Delight
> Veiled Melancholy has her sovran shrine,
> Though seen of none save him whose strenuous tongue
> Can burst Joy's grape against his palate fine;
>
> ('Ode on Melancholy') R.

*Bonfires celebrate and mark a conclusion (page 91).

There isn't enough in this book about the pleasures of bonfires. Sorry. R.

*Some gardens are even quite different in morning and evening (page 94).

Aren't they all? s.

* . . . the apparently timeless moment, perfectly poised, is of deepest importance to the contemplative gardener (page 95).

Is there a real distinction between the active and the contemplative gardener? Aren't all gardeners both, though more active at some moments and more contemplative at others? R.

*Here the restoration helps us to understand one moment in the development of taste and the history of our civilization (page 99).

I disagree. The slavish restoration of gardens of the past in all their detail seems to me an entirely pointless exercise. They are copies, wrenched out of historical context, part of the dreadful Heritage industry – though the study of garden history may be of minor scholarly interest and of course is a perfectly harmless activity. s.

Persons

There is a veiled implication throughout this chapter – and indeed it surfaces in other chapters – that the *real* gardener, who saves seed and takes cuttings and counts the day lost not mainly spent in greenhouse or herbaceous border, is a morally superior being and not just a better gardener. Rubbish. And that the person whose garden may be a joy to sit or walk in, but who does not do it all themselves, is somehow a lesser mortal.

Well, I love *gardens* – I am inspired by them, I love to see them, think of them, and be in them, and in my own best of all. But I hate much of the physical activity that has to be done in the garden and I don't feel ashamed of that. So long as my garden, which I plan in detail, gives me delight and delight to others, what matter? s.

* It is not only a surprising moment, it is a curiously exhilarating and releasing one (page 106).

Here Susan admires the disappointment of expectation which she deplored at the Painswick Rococo garden. Which just shows how narrow the line often is between success and failure in garden design. R.

* . . . her obscure little plants triumphed over Walter's vulgar dahlias (page 110).

What, pray, is so vulgar about a dahlia? No flowers are vulgar, only the way they are used. R.

* True gardeners, as opposed to exterior decorators (page 118).

I detect another sneer against those of us who are supposed not to be 'real gardeners'. s.

Senses

Thoughts of hamamelis (page 125).

Far too many plant names here.

   In fact, come to think of it, this is one of the things that puts so many people off gardening altogether. The English pay far too much attention to plants anyway, as well as all that business of growing and propagating, and the botanical minutiae. I like some plants – though there are a great many I don't like – but I care more for gardens as whole places than for individual plants. Plants are surely only a means to an end. s.

The White Garden at Sissinghurst has exercised a pernicious influence, particularly inexplicable since it is not the most successful area of that glorious garden (page 132).

Wider still and wider may the influence of the wonderful White Garden at Sissinghurst spread. It is the best bit. Before long all flowers in my own garden will be white. s.

Perhaps it is the quest for 'unusual plants' that is to blame (page 133).

Some plants have become 'unusual' because earlier gardeners, in their wisdom and good taste, didn't think them worth propagating. R.

Water

If a pool is not skilfully edged, the black butyl liner holding the water will be hideously visible (page 147).

It is also possible to go to the opposite extreme and hide the butyl liner with so much stone that the pond is diminished to a puddle. R.

Revisions

*. . . *but, provided you do it with care at the correct time, you can give your plants almost as peripatetic a life as the sofa and armchairs may enjoy indoors* (page 152).

Is there such a thing as a correct time? Autumn is usually the *best* time because the earth is warm and damp, and having shed its leaves the plant can concentrate on making roots. But many plants can be moved at any time if they are treated with sufficient care. Other plants – daphnes for example – hate being moved at all. R.

Things may require hard pruning, but is this the right moment for it? (page 153).

Again there may be a *best* time; the word 'right' has dreadful moral overtones and adds to gardening stress. Christopher Lloyd (whose books have taught me so much) writes in *The Well Tempered Garden* that he is 'a great believer in doing a job when I want to, and to hell with the consequences'. This may be a characteristically provocative overstatement, but let us consider what is the best time for us, not only for the plant. R.

Salvia patens (page 155).

I hesitate to make plant comments but I think this is rubbish. My garden is exposed, windswept and always several degrees colder than his, but I have *Salvia patens* growing very happily in a not especially sheltered spot. 'Always fly in the face of nature' seems to me to be a rather exciting motto for the gardener. S.

As the autumn sunlight thickens to a lemony milk and the first frosts are expected, the garden can still be interesting (page 156).

Of course it can. I hate all this sense of desperation come autumn and winter. Autumn is a time of wonderful decay, a slow slipping down into the bareness of winter, which is deeply satisfying. Why not enjoy it for what it is and stop the frantic search for yet more stuff that will flower – it only encourages the delusion that the garden year is everlasting (and perhaps the gardener immortal). S.

Sedums too will prolong the garden's interest (page 156).

Goodness, you must be desperate. This paragraph contains more hideous plants than the rest of the book. s.

. . . nerines (page 156).

There are many hideous plants but these seem to me to come pretty close to the top of the list. s.

It is amazing what garden structures can be 'mocked-up' out of the huge cardboard containers in which new washing machines and refrigerators are delivered (page 159).

For those who visit the junk yard less frequently, have no industrial polythene to hand, or who want to read their books and keep them, it may be easier to take photographs from key viewing points, have them enlarged and then draw in the new features (or get an artistic friend to draw them in for you). R.

Nothing is more depressing for a designer than to work for people who care so little about the garden that they will pronounce themselves delighted, whatever the proposed improvements (page 160).

I'm not sure how much this matters. Surely it's better they employ someone to improve the look of their garden than no one, since gardens can be an eyesore to an awful lot of people who have to look at them as they go by (which is not true of house interiors). s.